DISCOURSE ON METHOD

and MEDITATIONS

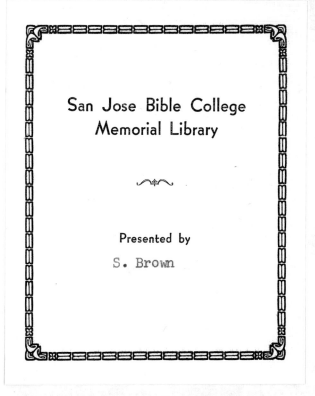

San Jose Bible College
Memorial Library

Presented by

S. Brown

The Library of Liberal Arts
OSKAR PIEST, FOUNDER

DISCOURSE
ON METHOD
and MEDITATIONS

Rene Descartes

Translated, with an introduction, by
Laurence J. Lafleur
Professor of Philosophy, The University of Akron

. . . .

The Library of Liberal Arts
published by
THE BOBBS-MERRILL COMPANY, INC.
A Subsidiary of Howard W. Sams & Co., Inc.
Indianapolis • New York

Rene Descartes: 1596-1650

DISCOURSE ON METHOD was originally published in 1637

MEDITATIONS was originally published in 1641

. . . .

CONTENTS

DISCOURSE ON THE METHOD OF RIGHTLY CONDUCTING THE REASON AND SEEKING TRUTH IN THE FIELD OF SCIENCE

THE MEDITATIONS
CONCERNING FIRST PHILOSOPHY

INTRODUCTION

Descartes' Place in History

By an almost universal agreement among philosophers and historians, René Descartes is considered the originator of modern philosophy, or at least the first important philosopher of our times. If we add to this the common belief that philosophy points the way for developments in all other fields, it will be evident that to Descartes is ascribed an importance comparable to that of the beginnings of intellectual culture in Greece or of the origin and spread of Christianity in the Mediterranean regions, and surpassing all other events in history. The study of Descartes can start in no more appropriate way than by inquiring into his reputation, and deciding in what sense and to what extent it is justified.

Descartes lived in a time of great change. The Mediaeval world was in the process of disintegration. The clergy had been divided for centuries into opposing factions following Thomas Aquinas, Duns Scotus, William of Occam, and others, and many individuals had been in practical revolt against the Church through an excessive interest in philosophy or science. Parts of the Church empire had fallen away through the rise of Protestantism; the Renaissance had recovered many of the ideas of Greek philosophy, exploration had stimulated interest in this world instead of the next, and the development of printing had disseminated knowledge much more widely than ever before.

The downfall of Mediaevalism is thus evidently not attributable to Descartes or to any combination of men or forces of the early seventeenth century, but rather stems from defects of Mediaevalism which had begun to appear centuries earlier. And if Descartes cannot be held responsible for the destruction of the old, it is almost equally absurd to hold him uniquely responsible for the new. Many men and many events were involved in determining what direction European civilization would take after Mediaevalism lost its hold: philosophers such as Roger Bacon, Francis Bacon, Hobbes, Machiavelli, and Montaigne; scientists such as Copernicus, Bruno, Kepler, and Galileo; religious reformers such as Wycliffe, Luther, and Calvin; events such as the discovery of the New World, the invention of the art of printing, and the rediscovery of Hellenic culture: all these and many more played roles that should not be obscured by the elevation of Descartes to prominence.

After all this has been admitted, however, it still remains true that Descartes contributed a great deal to modern culture: so much that he far surpasses any other individual or event, or even any small group of individuals or events, in the extent of his influence in determining the characteristics of modernism. The major elements of his influence may be grouped into six categories.

First, Descartes shared with many other individuals of his period a disbelief in authoritarianism and a belief in the unique adequacy of each individual's reason for the discovery of truth. On the negative side, Descartes is thus partly responsible for the decline of Roman Catholic authoritarianism, and for the development of anti-clericalism, particularly in France. On the positive side, he supports Protestantism in its affirmation of the supremacy of the individual conscience, and is one of the principal sources of democratic theory. Locke, for instance, developed the democratic tendency of Descartes by eliminating innate ideas, the only source from which a supernatural ethic might arise. Hume accepted Locke's ethical beliefs, and they were expanded into a coherent system of morality and political and economic theory by Bentham. In *The Meeting of East and West,* Northrop has argued at some length that modern America must be understood in the light of Locke's ideas, modern England largely in terms of those of Bentham. French political theory, similarly, has been greatly influenced by the French philosophers of the Enlightenment, who were in turn strongly influenced both by Descartes directly and by the English school already mentioned.

Second on our list is Descartes' rationalism and scientific optimism. The world, he is sure, is essentially rational and comprehensible, so that the task of philosophy can be accomplished; and with the proper effort on the part of an individual philosopher, no doubt, will be. We thus find philosophers over a period of two and a half centuries building systems which they are optimistically certain are close to the absolute truth. The task of science can also be accomplished, and the world thereby turned into a utopia: Descartes thought he might even achieve this result in his own lifetime. The belief that science can regenerate the world has been characteristic of all the modern periods: the belief that science's final success is just around the corner was characteristic of the modern period until late in the nineteenth century. Even some of the specific methods of modern science are proclaimed by Descartes: he insisted that all laws must be universal, and eventually derivable from a single basic law of the universe. Therefore scientific progress is to be achieved not only, or even primarily, by learning new facts, but rather by the device of consolidating laws already achieved in different fields, as, for example, Newton combined Galileo's laws of falling bodies with Kepler's laws of planetary motions. But the first outstanding achievement in combining laws was that of Descartes himself when he combined the methods of algebra and geometry in the new field of analytic geometry. The importance of this achievement is difficult to overestimate, for it not only served as an example of the possibilities of the new scientific method and as a spur to men's enthusiasm, but also laid the foundation for the growth of mathematics in modern times. From analytic geometry came the simultaneous discovery of the calculus by Leibniz and Newton, and on the calculus is based the whole superstructure of modern developments in mathematics and of its application to the understanding of nature.

The third field of Cartesian influence is the approach to philosophy through the analysis of experience. To us this approach seems so natural that it is hard to realize that it need not have been used. The Greeks and Romans, for example, derived little of philosophical value from such an approach: only those of sceptical inclination used it. After Descartes, on the other hand, it produced association psychology in England, was continually found in English and Continental philosophies, and was expressed in such art forms as pointillism and such literary forms as the poetry of Browning or the novels of James Joyce. To continue this list is much too easy: reasons could be found for adding to it an endless number of the ideas and products of the last few centuries.

Fourthly, Descartes' proof of the existence of the self raised the question of what that certainly-existing self really is. There is clearly no evidence in Descartes' argument that this self is immortal, and we thus encounter a recrudescence of interest in the search for logical or empirical evidence of immortality. Historically more important than this, there is no certainty that the self is identical throughout a lifetime, or even that there is only one existing at a time. This result of the Cartesian philosophy was not immediately evident, since men were generally predisposed by their religious backgrounds to accept Descartes' position uncritically, and it was only around the beginning of the twentieth century that evidence of amnesia and multiple personality shocked a tradition-minded world into a scientific re-examination of the nature of personality and personal identity.

The fifth way in which Descartes was influential was in his expression of metaphysical dualism. This has become so thoroughly a part of our intellectual heritage that the man with no philosophical training whatsoever thinks along these lines and finds the Cartesian philosophy obvious to the extent that he may consider all other philosophies perverse distortions of the self-evident truth. In philosophy proper, Cartesian dualism has been important because of its difficulties: how can two fundamentally unlike entities compose a universe that is so obviously well integrated, especially since almost all philosophers and scientists are committed to the view that explanation consists in showing that a multitude of dissimilar events are in fact alike? And how can mind, which is not spatial, cause a particle of matter to move from one location to another; or how can matter, which is unable to do anything but move in space, produce an idea? Answers to this problem were attempted at three levels: the scientific, the cosmological, and the ontological, although the three were interrelated in their development.

On the scientific level, Descartes believed that the quantity of motion remained unchanged, but that mind could change the direction in which the motion took place. It soon became evident, however, that this would violate other physical laws than the conservation of the quantity of motion, since change of direction results from the application of force, since action and reaction are equal and opposite, and for a variety of other reasons. Thus the explanation of how mind affected matter became more and more elaborate and indirect as scientific knowledge increased. But, fundamentally, no explanation, however intricate, would serve. For the basic assumption of science is that a necessary and sufficient cause can be found for any phenomenon. The conception held by science until very recently was that the necessary and sufficient cause would also be rational—that is, that its nature would be such that its action could be logically derived from it. But if Descartes' metaphysical dualism is correct, there can be no rational cause of a physical event except another physical event; and this philosophical notion is powerfully supported by the fact that a physical scientist, using tools which are basically extensions of the sense organs, could not observe a non-physical cause if such existed. The equally logical prejudice against physical efficacy in mental occurrences never developed, because psychology and the social sciences were comparative latecomers and lacked the prestige of the physical sciences. So modern science has developed with strong prejudices not only against Divine intervention in the natural order, but also against mental causes being efficacious in physical affairs, and even, by extension, against the existence of any unproved mental phenomena. Regardless of facts pro or con, therefore, there has been a violent antipathy to mental telepathy, multiple personality, and hypnosis. More directly consequent upon the theory is the objection to telekinesis. In the field of psychology, the implication has been that ideas and volitions have no efficacy, and that brain states must be substituted for mental states in psychological laws. But this in turn has further implications. While for Descartes the mental world was of equal importance with the physical, the mind has now come to be considered incapable of producing or explaining its own states. It remains as a fact, but as a wholly unimportant fact. Behaviorism is the natural consequence, and the redefinition of psychology in terms of stimulus-response, or organismic-environmental interrelationships. In biology the theory has led to the assumption that mental traits are not hereditary: all apparent instances of that sort are attributed to the inheritance of some unknown predisposing physiological structure. It should be noted that all these prejudices are derived in part from Cartesian dualism, and that there is nothing in scientific theory or method, taken alone, to account for them. All that is scientifically demanded is that some causal explanation be found for any event, not that the cause should be physical in nature. Furthermore, the resulting doctrine of materialism or epiphenomenalism, which has always been intellectually unattractive, has been rendered meaningless by the developments in physics in the twentieth century.

On the cosmological level, Descartes' own answer to the difficulty of interaction was a simple and obviously inadequate statement that in the beginning God had willed it so. Apart from the fact that such a *Deus ex machina* explains nothing by its very broadness, it is not evident what advantage exists in a rational God's behaving irrationally over nature behaving irrationally. Descartes' theory was elaborated by Geulinx and other Cartesians on the Continent to make God continuously responsible for all interaction. Another possible answer on the cosmological level is the denial that interaction occurs, so that the appearance of it is an illusion due to a perfect parallelism between the mental and the physical. This idea was developed by Leibniz.

Inextricably interwoven with the cosmological level is the ontological level, where the problem of dualism is met by denying dualism. One atypical conclusion is neutral monism: the denial that matter and mind are different. This was proposed in very different ways by Leibniz and Spinoza. Much later we find pluralism and modern realism developed to answer the same problem. But the more typical conclusion is that matter does not exist: Berkeley is the most prominent representative of this conclusion, but even Malebranche and Leibniz can be readily interpreted as idealists, and idealism soon became the most popular form of philosophy. Thus Descartes' dualism led naturally both to the materialistic tendency in science and to the idealistic trend in philosophy.

The sixth and last field in which Descartes' influence was prominent was epistemology. Here there are two theories of importance to be considered. First is the correspondence theory of truth, according to which at least some kinds of ideas are correct insofar as they are good copies of external reality. Second is a threefold source of knowledge. Knowledge, according to Descartes, may be obtained intuitively, on the ground that we have clear and distinct conceptions which must be true. Notice that conceptions are in question, not perceptions: the clear and distinct knowledge which we have of the external world is scientific knowledge, not the acceptance of appearances. But appearances, or empirical data, are clearly another source of information, including introspection and internal bodily feeling as well as the external senses. And when we possess some knowledge, other knowledge may be obtained from it by inference. Now these three methods of obtaining knowledge are not necessarily independent. If we eliminate from consideration both revealed truth and Descartes' arguments for the existence of God, which involve a quite special problem, it is easy to maintain that intuition, or the clear and distinct idea, always operates in terms of an immediate datum or in terms of inference. Thus the empirical and rational avenues to truth may be no more than two sub-divisions of Descartes' logical method. If this is not so, in-tuition becomes a mystical *a priori* and is just as dangerous in epistemology, and for the same reason, as the concept of a *Deus ex machina* is in metaphysics. But whether or not Descartes did or would reject such a mystical intuition, it was clearly opposed to some elements in his philosophy, and it was a quite natural step for Locke to disown it utterly. Locke went too far, however, and left all knowledge in greater jeopardy than it had been left by Descartes, as was made clear by Berkeley and Hume. For on Descartes' correspondence theory, an idea could only be an adequate copy of another idea, never of the wholly different physical world, so that Berkeley's sub-jective idealism is the logical result. Further analysis shows that ideas are also debarred from being copies of thinking be-ings or of God, so that even Berkeley's position must give way to the sceptical conclusions of Hume. Locke's philosophy made this derivation inevitable by abandoning a possible escape that Descartes devised; Descartes only claimed that *some* ideas are to be evaluated in terms of correspondence. In addition, Locke provides a still more direct path to Hume's scepticism: if all knowledge is sense data, then clearly we can have no knowledge of anything but sense data, and physical substance, mental substance, and logical rules must be out-lawed. Finally, the problem thus posed, Hume's solution to which is clearly unacceptable, leads to Kant, subsequent Ger-man idealism, and the modern tendency to take problems of methodology, in science and philosophy, as prior to all other considerations.

The Discourse on Method

The first work that Descartes completed and published was the *Discourse on Method* together with its appended essays, *Optics, Meteorology,* and *Geometry.* The full title of the prin-cipal essay is the *Discourse on the Method of Rightly Con-*

ducting the Reason and Seeking Truth in the Sciences, and in this work he is in effect proclaiming that he has discovered a method that will enable anyone, however modest his abilities may be, to discover any truth that it is possible for a human being to discover. But the *Discourse* does not go into much detail in describing this method, for which we have to go to the uncompleted *Rules for the Direction of the Mind.* Rather, the *Discourse* and its attendant essays appear to constitute a prospectus: Descartes had accomplished much already, but had much more to do, and in order to have some chance of completing the task in his own lifetime he needed to carry on the necessary experiments. Anyone interested in knowledge and in the public welfare is invited to contribute: "Here is the method," he says in effect, "which I have discovered; and here, in *Optics, Meteorology,* and *Geometry,* are a few samples to show how successful this method has been in my hands. If you will invest in me, I can give you similar successes elsewhere—perhaps, in fine, the key to nature and human happiness." And so, in order to understand the *Discourse on Method,* we will do well to examine the exhibits which go with it.

Part of the *Discourse on Method* is devoted to an outline of the philosophy which Descartes later describes in greater detail in the *Meditations on First Philosophy,* and we have already indicated its pervasive influence on modern times. We have also mentioned his *Geometry,* the importance of which can hardly be overestimated. For it was not only the beginning of a new field of mathematics, and destined to become the mainstay of all modern mathematical development, but it was also the first important mathematical discovery since Greek times, and a stimulus to further thought in that field. In addition, it offered a needed example of the possibility of achievement in mathematics; it furnished the suggestion that further progress in any line of thought might depend upon the integration of separate bits of knowledge already available; and it turned out to be an ideal vehicle for the analysis of motion.

Descartes' more specifically scientific achievements are divided among the *Discourse on Method, Optics,* and *Meteorology*—the latter two essays, however, deal more concretely with scientific problems. Descartes' anatomy is accurate enough, but he makes heat the cause rather than the result of bodily motion. Nevertheless, though Descartes is so mistaken in the functioning of the body, his picture is not altogether impossible, and foreshadows to some extent the principle of the steam engine and the internal combustion engine.

The principal achievements presented by Descartes in *Optics* are the following: the statement of the wave theory of light; the vector analysis of motion; the law of sines in refraction; the first theoretical account of far-sightedness and near-sightedness; the first adequate account of space-perception; the first adequate account of the theory of lenses; the first recognition of spherical aberration and of the method of correcting it; the determination of light-gathering power in a telescope; the principle of the iris diaphragm; the draw-tube; the telescopic finder; the use of illuminating equipment in conjunction with the microscope; and the parabolic mirror.

His achievements in *Meteorology* include the following: he rejects Divine intervention as the explanation of events; he states the kinetic theory of heat, and foreshadows Charles's law, and the concept of specific heat; he gives the first outline of a scientific meteorology in his treatment of winds, clouds, and precipitation; he gives a correct and accurate description and explanation of the primary, secondary, and reflection rainbows; and he describes the division of white light into colors by a prism, and sets up the apparatus of the slit spectroscope.

Meditations on First Philosophy

The *Discourse on Method, Optics, Meteorology,* and *Geometry* were published in 1637, but had been written quite some time earlier, some parts at least ten years earlier. The *Meditations* were published in 1641, but although some of it was no doubt written earlier, probably none of it antedated the *Discourse*. Thus the four-year interval in the time of publication of the two works represents a much longer interval in the time of writing; and although there are very few differences in the doctrines proclaimed by Descartes before and after this interval, there is a world of difference in his attitude.

Descartes is not only the father of modern philosophy, of modern mathematics, and of modern physics, optics, meteorology, and science generally, but also the child of the Middle Ages. The ideas of Aristotle and of Mediaeval philosophy are so deeply ingrained in him that they are never really questioned; they govern the pattern of his thinking even when he does not consciously admit them and they are openly espoused during the development of his thought as the dictates of the light of nature. So in Descartes there were two competing tendencies: he was at once the progressive, or rather the radical intellectual rebel, ready to break away from Mediaevalism and the Church to lay the foundation of a new philosophy and to build his hopes for the future of mankind on the development of science in general and of medicine in particular; and at the same time he was the conservative, educated in the Mediaeval tradition of the Jesuit order.

It is a matter of common experience that older persons tend more to conservatism; for this reason alone it is not strange that the Descartes of 1641 should have been more conservative than the Descartes of 1637 and earlier. But there was a more telling reason for the change. The Descartes of 1637 and before, while not actually unknown, had published nothing. His teachers, friends, and acquaintances recognized his abilities and expected great things of him, but as much can be said of countless men in every generation. Would this expectation be fulfilled? Born in 1596, Descartes was not so young any more, and doubts may have arisen in the minds of his friends and perhaps even in his own. Descartes tells us himself, in the *Discourse,* that someone has circulated the rumor that his philosophy was completed. His situation was like that later described by Daudet: he ran the risk of being compared to *"lou fusiou de mestre Gervaï,"* and like Daudet's hero Tartarin, he willingly faced dangers to avoid losing not only his reputation but also his self-esteem.

In 1641, the situation was completely changed; the writings of 1637 had achieved a tremendous *éclat* and had established Descartes' reputation throughout Europe. He was honored and deferred to in philosophic, scientific, and theological circles. From having everything to gain and nothing to lose, his position had changed to that of having nothing to gain and everything to lose. Why then antagonize the Church, the most powerful force in Europe?

It is therefore noteworthy that Descartes' later works show important differences from his earlier. Not that his philosophy had changed, but the emphasis had shifted. Those issues in which he was in agreement with the Church were stressed, and the points of disagreement completely overlooked. Certainly there are no passages in the *Meditations* comparable to those in the *Discourse on Method,* in which Descartes' allegiance to Church doctrine is proclaimed, in the translator's opinion, in a way which must leave some doubt as to whether Descartes really accepted the priority of established doctrine over his own new insights. The choice of language also is indicative; Descartes now writes in Latin, the language of the Church, of the Middle Ages, of the conservative intellectuals; instead of in French, as formerly, with the consequent appeal to fewer clergy and more lay readers.

In science, too, the change is notable. The later Descartes has few new theories to offer—nothing certainly to compare with his great fecundity of earlier years—and even these are largely developments of ideas that appeared in his earlier work. Of his later theories, the most important is the statement of what is now known as Newton's first law of motion. Next in importance is the theory of vortices, which was scientifically inaccurate and apparently conceived in the hope of reconciling Galileo's concept of the solar system with the *homo*-centric position of the Church, by means of a primitive theory of relativity. At the same time Descartes affirms the nonexistence of void, which logically leads to the conclusion that the propagation of light is instantaneous, in contradiction to his earlier view.

Thus the Descartes of the *Meditations* is both philosophically and scientifically less advanced than the Descartes of the *Discourse on Method*. Yet, while the *Method* is historically more significant, the *Meditations* have been traditionally rated Descartes' most important philosophic work, and from the point of view of philosophical content rather than historical significance, this is undoubtedly the case. The *Meditations* contain the most thorough exposition and defense of Descartes' philosophy, and it is in this work that he most clearly indicates the presuppositions, mainly taken from scholasticism, upon which his reasoning is based. Whether the reader agrees or disagrees with a particular argument, he is sure to find the reading of the *Meditations* a challenging experience and one of the most rewarding studies in all the great literature of philosophy.

LAURENCE J. LAFLEUR

NOTE ON THE TEXT

The translation of the *Discourse on Method* was made from the original French text and later revised to take into consideration the Latin text of 1644. In fact, it seemed advisable to adhere rather more closely to the Latin than the French, since Descartes wrote of it:

> These treatises, which I wrote in French and published seven years ago, were recently translated into Latin by a friend of mine [1] and his version intrusted to me so that I might alter anything that did not suit me. This I have done in several places, but I may have missed many others. My changes may be distinguished from his by the fact that he has everywhere tried to give a faithful word-for-word translation, whereas I have often changed the meanings themselves, and have everywhere attempted to improve, not his words, but my meaning.

The headings for the Parts of the *Discourse* were inserted by the Translator and were taken from the first paragraph of the *Discourse* where Descartes enumerates the parts of his work. For the explanation of half-brackets and half-parentheses, see the note on the *Meditations*.

The translation of the *Meditations* is taken from three sources: the second Latin edition of 1642, which was the first one printed from Descartes' own manuscript and under his own supervision, the first French translation of 1647 by the Duc de Luynes, but read and approved by Descartes, and the second French translation by Clerselier. An attempt has been made in this translation to integrate these three versions into one complete and accurate edition by the use of brackets and parentheses. The reader may, by omitting the parentheses and brackets, have a translation which contains all ideas in the three versions. By omitting bracketed material, he will have a

[1] Etienne De Courcelles.

translation essentially that of the original Latin, and by omitting material in parentheses, that of the first French edition.

( )   indicates where the Latin adds a word or phrase not found in the French.

⌈ ⌉   indicates where the first French version adds a word or phrase not found in the Latin.

( )⌈ ⌉   indicates where the two versions differ. The Latin enclosed in the parentheses; the first French enclosed in square brackets. A connective such as "and" or "or" is occasionally supplied and the brackets and parentheses overlap so as to include it.

⌈( )⌉   indicates material occurring for the first time in the second French edition.

The numbers enclosed in brackets and parentheses refer to the corresponding pages in the French and Latin texts of the Adam and Tannery editions.

For the *Discourse,* the numbers enclosed in parentheses refer to the Latin edition of 1644; the numbers enclosed in brackets, to the first French edition.

For the *Meditations,* the numbers enclosed in parentheses refer to the second Latin text; the numbers enclosed in brackets, to the first French text.

The separate edition of *Meditations* previously published in the Library of Liberal Arts may be referred to for a discussion of some of the problems of interpretation and translation.

L. J. L.

SELECTED BIBLIOGRAPHY

DESCARTES' MAJOR WORKS

Discours de la méthode (1637).

Dioptrique (1637).

La Géométrie (1637).

Les Météores (1637).

Meditationes de prima philosophia (1641).

Principia philosophiae (1644).

Oeuvres de Descartes, publiées par Charles Adam et Paul Tannery sous les auspices du Ministère de l'instruction publique. Paris, 1897-1913.

COLLATERAL READING

Balz, A. G., *Descartes and the Modern Mind.* Yale University, 1952.

———, *Cartesian Studies.* Columbia University, 1951.

Brunschwicg, Léon, *Descartes et Pascal, lecteurs de Montaigne.* Paris and New York, 1944.

———, *René Descartes.* Paris, 1937.

Cajori, Florian, *Ce que Newton doit à Descartes.* Paris, 1926.

Cresson, André, *Descartes; sa vie, son oeuvre.* Paris, 1942.

Fischer, Kuno, *Descartes and His School.* London, 1887.

Gibson, A. Boyce, *The Philosophy of Descartes.* London, 1932.

Gilson, Étienne, *Le rôle de la pensée médiévale dans la formation du système cartésien.* Paris, 1930.

———, *La doctrine cartésienne de la liberté et la théologie.* Paris, 1913.

Iverach, James, *Descartes, Spinoza and the New Philosophy.* New York, 1904.

Jascolevich, Alejandro A., *Three Conceptions of Mind. Their Bearing on the Denaturalization of the Mind in History.* New York, 1926.

Keeling, S. V., *Descartes.* London, 1934.

Kemp Smith, Norman, *New Studies in the Philosophy of Descartes*. London, 1953.

Laporte, Jean Marie Frédéric, *Le rationalisme de Descartes*. Paris, 1945.

Lévy-Bruhl, L., *History of Modern Philosophy in France*. Chicago, 1899.

Maritain, Jacques, *Three Reformers: Luther, Descartes, Rousseau*. New York, 1937.

Mouy, Paul, *Le développement de la physique cartésienne, 1646-1712*. Paris, 1934.

Roy, Jean H., *L'imagination selon Descartes*. Paris, 1944.

Scott, J. F., *The Scientific Work of René Descartes*. London, 1953.

Tellier, Auguste, *Descartes et la médecine*. Paris, 1928.

Vartanian, A., *Diderot and Descartes*. Princeton University, 1953.

Versfeld, Marthinus, *An Essay on the Metaphysics of Descartes*. London, 1940.

DISCOURSE ON THE METHOD OF RIGHTLY
CONDUCTING THE REASON AND SEEKING
TRUTH IN THE FIELD OF SCIENCE

DISCOURSE ON THE METHOD
OF
RIGHTLY CONDUCTING THE REASON
AND SEEKING TRUTH IN
THE SCIENCES

If this discourse seems too long to be read at one sitting, it may be divided into six parts. In the first will be found various thoughts on the sciences; in the second, the principal rules of the method the author has used; in the third, some moral rules derived from this method; in the fourth, his proofs of the existence of God and of the human soul which form the basis of his philosophy; in the fifth are treated some questions of physics, especially the explanation of the heartbeat and of some other difficulties in medicine, as well as the difference between the souls of men and animals; and in the last, some prerequisites for further advances in the study of nature, as well as the author's reasons for writing this work.

PART ONE

SOME THOUGHTS ON THE SCIENCES

Good sense is mankind's most equitably divided endowment, for everyone thinks that he is so abundantly provided with it that [2] even those ⸝with the most insatiable appetites and⸜ most difficult to please in other ways do not usually want more than they have of this. As it is not likely that everyone is mistaken, this evidence shows that the ability to judge correctly, and to distinguish the true from the false—which is really what is meant by good sense or reason—is the same by ⌐innate¬ nature in all men; and that differences of opinion are not due to differences in intelligence, but merely to the fact that we use different approaches and consider different things. For it is not enough to have a good mind: one must use it well. The greatest souls are capable of the greatest vices as well as of the greatest virtues; and those who walk slowly can, if they follow the right path, go much farther than those who run rapidly in the wrong direction.

As for myself, I have never supposed that my mind was above the ordinary. On the contrary, I have often wished to have as quick a wit or as clear and distinct an imagination, or as ready and retentive a memory, as another person. And I know of no other qualities which make for a good mind, because as far as reason is concerned, it is the only thing which makes us men ⌐and distinguishes us from the animals¬, and I am therefore satisfied that it is fully present in each one of us. In this I follow the general opinion (541) of philosophers, who say that there are differences in degree only in the [3] *accidental* qualities, and not in the *essential* qualities or natures of individuals of the same species.

But I do not hesitate to claim the good fortune of having stumbled, in my youth, upon certain paths which led me without difficulty ⌐to certain considerations and maxims from which I formed a method of gradually increasing my knowledge ⌐and of improving my abilities¬ as much as the mediocrity of my talents and the shortness of my life will permit. For I have already had such results that although in self-judgment I try to lean toward undervaluation ⌐rather than to presumption¬, I cannot escape a feeling of extreme satisfaction with the progress I believe I have already made in the search for truth. And although from the philosophers' viewpoint almost all the activities of men appear to me as vain and useless, yet I conceive such hopes for the future that if some single one of the occupations of men, as men, should be truly good and important, I dare to believe that it is the one I have chosen.

It is always possible that I am wrong, and that I am mistaking a bit of copper and glass for gold and diamonds. I know how subject we are to making false judgments in things that concern ourselves, and how much we ought to mistrust the judgments of our friends when they are in our own favor. But I should be glad to show in this *Discourse* [4] what are the paths I have taken 'to search for truth,' and to present a sketch of my 'whole' life, so that each one can form his own judgment of it. In this way I may learn from the opinions of those who read it, and thus add another to the methods of progress which I am accustomed to use.

So it is not my intention to present a method which everyone ought to follow in order to think well, but only to show how I have made the attempt myself. Those who counsel others must consider themselves superior to those whom they counsel, and if they fall short in the least detail they are 'much' to blame. I only propose this writing as an autobiography, or, if you prefer, as a story in which you may possibly find some examples of conduct which you might see fit to imitate, as well as several others which you would have no reason to follow. I hope that it will prove useful to some without being harmful to any, and that all will take my frankness kindly.

From my childhood I lived in a world of books, and since I was taught that by their help I could gain a clear and assured knowledge of everything useful in life, (542) I was eager to learn from them. But as soon as I had finished the course of studies which usually admits one to the ranks of the learned, I changed my opinion completely. For I found myself saddled with so many doubts and errors that I seemed to have gained nothing in trying to educate myself unless it was to discover more and more fully how ignorant I was.

Nevertheless [5] I had been in one of the most celebrated schools in 'all of' Europe, where I thought there should be wise men if wise men existed anywhere on earth. I had learned there everything that others learned, and, not satisfied with merely the knowledge that was taught, I had perused as many books as I could find which contained more unusual and recondite knowledge. I also knew the opinions of others about myself, and that I was in no way judged inferior to my fellow students, even though several of them were preparing to become professors. And finally, it did not seem to me that our own times were less flourishing and fertile than were any of the earlier periods. All this led me to conclude that I could judge others by myself, and to decide that there was no such wisdom in the world as I had previously hoped to find.

I did not, however, cease to value the disciplines of the schools. I knew that the languages which one learns there are necessary to understand the works of the ancients; and that the delicacy of fiction 'refines and' enlivens the mind; that famous deeds of history ennoble it and, if read with understanding, aid in maturing one's judgment; that the reading of all the great books is like conversing with the best people of earlier times: it is even a studied conversation in which the authors show us only the best of their thoughts; that eloquence has incomparable powers and beauties; that poetry has [6] enchanting delicacy and sweetness; that mathematics has very subtle processes which can serve as much to satisfy the inquiring mind as to aid all the arts and to diminish man's labor; that treatises on morals contain very useful teachings and exhortations to virtue; that theology teaches us how to go to heaven; that philosophy teaches us to talk with an appearance of truth about all things, and to make ourselves admired by the less learned; that law, medicine, and the other sciences bring honors and wealth to those who pursue them; and finally, that it is desirable to have examined all of them, even to the most (543) superstitious and false, in order to recognize their real worth and avoid being deceived thereby.

But I thought that I had already spent enough time on languages, and even on reading the works of the ancients, and their histories and fiction. For conversing with the ancients is much like traveling. It is good to know something of the customs of various peoples, in order to judge our own more objectively, and so that we do not make the mistake of the untraveled in supposing that everything contrary to our customs is ridiculous and irrational. But when one spends too much time traveling, one becomes at last a stranger at home; and those who are too interested in things which occurred in past centuries are often remarkably ignorant of what is going on today. In addition, fiction makes us imagine a number of events [7] as possible which are really impossible, and even the most faithful histories, if they do not alter or embroider episodes to make them more worth reading, almost always omit the meanest and least illustrious circumstances so that the remainder is distorted. Thus it happens that those who regulate their behavior by the examples they find in books are apt to fall into the extravagances of the knights of romances, and undertake projects which it is beyond their ability to complete ⟨or hope for things beyond their destiny⟩.

I esteemed eloquence highly, and loved poetry, but I felt that both were gifts of nature rather than fruits of study. Those who reason most cogently, and work over their thoughts to make them clear and intelligible, are always the most persuasive, even if they speak only a provincial dialect and have never studied rhetoric. Those who have the most agreeable imaginations and can express their thoughts with the most grace and color cannot fail to be the best poets, even if the poetic art is unknown to them.

I was especially pleased with mathematics, because of the certainty and self-evidence of its proofs; but I did not yet see its true usefulness and, thinking that it was good only for the mechanical arts, I was astonished that nothing more noble had been built on so firm and solid a foundation. On the other hand, I compared the ethical writings of the ancient pagans to [8] very superb and magnificent palaces built only on mud and sand: they laud the virtues and ⟨rightly⟩ make them appear more desirable than anything else in the world; (544) but they give no adequate criterion of virtue, and often what they call by such a name is nothing but ⟨cruelty and⟩ apathy, parricide, pride or despair.

I revered our theology, and hoped as much as anyone else to get to heaven, but having learned on great authority that the road was just as open to the most ignorant as to the most learned, and that the truths of revelation which lead thereto are beyond our understanding, I would not have dared to submit them to the weakness of my reasonings. I thought that to succeed in their examination it would be necessary to have some extraordinary assistance from heaven, and to be more than a man.

I will say nothing of philosophy except that it has been studied for many centuries by the most outstanding minds without having produced anything which is not in dispute and consequently doubtful ⸢and uncertain⸥. I did not have enough presumption to hope to succeed better than the others; and when I noticed how many different opinions learned men may hold on the same subject, despite the fact that no more than one of them can ever be right, I resolved to consider almost as false any opinion which was merely plausible.

Finally, when it came to the other branches of learning, since they took their cardinal principles from philosophy, I judged [9] that nothing solid could have been built on so insecure a foundation. Neither the honor nor the profit to be gained thereby sufficed to make me study them, for I was fortunately not in such a financial condition as to make it necessary to trade upon my learning; and though I was not enough of a cynic to despise fame, I was little concerned with that which I could only obtain on false pretenses ⸢, that is, by claiming to know things that were in fact false⸥. And finally, I thought I knew enough of the disreputable doctrines not to be taken in by the promises of an alchemist, the predictions of an astrologer, the impostures of a magician, or by the tricks and boasts of any of those who profess to know that which they do not know.

This is why I gave up my studies entirely as soon as I reached the age when I was no longer under the control of my teachers. I resolved to seek no other knowledge than that which I might find within myself, or perhaps in the great book of nature. I ⸢then⸥ spent a few (545) years ⸢of my adolescence⸥ traveling, seeing courts and armies, living with people of diverse types and stations of life, acquiring varied experience, testing myself in the episodes which fortune sent me, and, above all, thinking about the things around me so that I could derive some profit from them. For it seemed to me that I might find much more of the truth in the cogitations which each man made on things which were important to him, and where [10] he would be the loser if he judged badly, than in the cogitations of a man of letters in his study, concerned with speculations which produce no effect, and which have no consequences to him except perhaps that the farther they are removed from common sense, the more they titillate his vanity, since then he needs so much more wit and skill to make them seem plausible. Besides, I was always eager to learn to distinguish truth from falsehood, so that I could make intelligent decisions about the affairs of this life ⟨and act with greater confidence⟩.

It is true that while I did nothing but observe the customs of other men, I found nothing there to satisfy me, and I noted just about as much difference of opinion as I had previously remarked among philosophers. The greatest profit to me was, therefore, that I became acquainted with customs generally approved and accepted by other great peoples that would appear extravagant and ridiculous among ourselves, and so I learned not to believe too firmly what I learned only from example and custom. Also I gradually freed myself from many errors which could ⌈obscure the light of nature and⌉ make us less capable of correct reasoning. But after spending several years in thus studying the book of nature and acquiring experience, I eventually reached the decision to study my own self, and to employ all my abilities to try to choose the right path. This produced much [11] better results in my case, I think, than would have been produced if I had never left my books and my country.

PART TWO

THE PRINCIPAL RULES OF THE METHOD

I was then in Germany, where I had gone because of ⌐the desire to see⌐ the wars which are still not ended; and while I was returning to the army from the coronation of the Emperor, I was caught by the onset of winter. There was no conversation to occupy me, and being untroubled by any cares or passions, I remained all day alone in a warm room. There I had plenty of leisure to examine my ideas. One of the first that occurred to me was that frequently there is less perfection in a work produced by several persons (546) than in one produced by a single hand. Thus we notice that buildings conceived and completed by a single architect are usually more beautiful and better planned than those remodeled by several persons using ancient walls ⌐of various vintages⌐ ⌐that had originally been built for quite other purposes⌐ ⌐along with new ones⌐. Similarly, those ancient towns which were originally nothing but hamlets, and in the course of time have become great cities, are ordinarily very badly arranged compared to one of the symmetrical metropolitan districts which a city planner has laid out on an open plain according to his own designs. It is true that when we consider their buildings one by one, there is often as much beauty in the first city as in the second, or even more; nevertheless, when we observe how they are arranged, here a large unit, there a small; and how the streets are crooked and uneven, one [12] would rather suppose that chance and not the decisions of rational men had so arranged them. And when we consider that there were always some officials in charge of private building, whose duty it was to see that they were conducive to the general good appearance of the city, we recognize that it is not easy to do a good job when using only the works of others. Similarly I supposed that peoples who were once half savage ⌐and barbarous⌐, and who became civilized by a gradual process and invented their laws one by one as the harmfulness of crimes and quarrels forced them to outlaw them, would be less well governed than those who have followed the constitutions of some prudent legislator from the time that their communities were founded. Thus it is quite certain that the condition of the true religion, whose rules were laid down by God alone, must be incomparably superior to all others. And, to speak of human affairs, I believe that Sparta was such a flourishing community, not because of the goodness of each of its laws in particular, seeing that many of them were very strange and even contrary to good morals, but because they were produced by a single legislator, and so all tended to the same end. And similarly I thought that the sciences found in books, at least those whose reasons were only probable and which had no proofs, have grown up little by little by the accumulation of the opinions of many different persons, and are therefore by no means as near to the truth as the simple and natural reasonings of a man [13] ⌐of good sense⌐ ⌐, laboring under no prejudice⌐ concerning the things which he experiences.

Likewise I thought that we were all children before (547) being men, at which time we were necessarily under the control of our appetites and our teachers, and that neither of these influences is wholly consistent, and neither of them, perhaps, always tends toward the better. It is therefore impossible that our judgments should be as pure and firm as they would have been had we the ⌐whole⌐ use of our ⌐mature⌐ reason from the time of our birth and if we had never been under any other control.

It is true that we never tear down all the houses in a city just to rebuild them in a different way and to make the streets more beautiful; but we do see that individual owners often have theirs torn down and rebuilt, and even that they may be forced to do so ⌐when the building is crumbling with age, or⌐ when ⌐the foundation is not firm and⌐ it is in danger of collapsing. By this example I was convinced that a private individual should not seek to reform a nation by changing all its

customs and destroying it to construct it anew, nor to reform
the body of knowledge or the system of education. Nevertheless, as far as the opinions which I had been receiving since
my birth were concerned, I could not do better than to reject them completely for once in my lifetime, and to resume
them afterwards, or perhaps accept better ones in their place,
when I had [14] determined how they fitted into a rational
scheme. And I firmly believed that by this means I would
succeed in conducting my life much better than if I built only
upon the old foundations and gave credence to the principles
which I had acquired in my childhood without ever having
examined them to see whether they were true or not. For
though I noticed several difficulties in the way, they were
neither insurmountable nor comparable to those involved in
the slightest reform of public affairs. For public affairs are on
a large scale, and large edifices are too difficult to set up again
once they have been thrown down, too difficult even to pre-
serve once they have been shaken, and their fall is necessarily
catastrophic. It is certain that many institutions have defects,
since their differences alone guarantee that much, but custom
has no doubt inured us to many of them. Custom has perhaps
even found ways to avoid or correct more defects than prudence could have done. Finally, present institutions are practically always more tolerable than would be a change in them;
just as highways which twist and turn among the mountains
become gradually so easy to travel, as a result of much use,
that it is much better to follow them than to attempt to go
more directly by climbing cliffs and descending to the bottom
of precipices. (548)

That is why I cannot at all approve those mischievous spirits
who, not being called either by birth or by attainments to a
position of political power, are nevertheless constantly proposing some new [15] reform. If I thought the slightest basis could
be found in this *Discourse* for a suspicion that I was guilty of
this folly, I would be loath to permit it to be published. Never
has my intention been more than to try to reform my own
ideas, and rebuild them on foundations that would be wholly

mine. If my building has pleased me sufficiently to display a model of it to the public, it is not because I advise anyone to copy it. Those whom God has more bountifully endowed will no doubt have higher aims; there are others, I fear, for whom my own are too adventurous. Even the decision to abandon all one's preconceived notions is not an example for all to follow, and the world is largely composed of two sorts of individuals who should not try to follow it. First, there are those who think themselves more able than they really are, and so make precipitate judgments and do not have enough patience to think matters through thoroughly. From this it follows that once they have taken the liberty of doubting their established principles, thus leaving the highway, they will never be able to keep to the narrow path which must be followed to go more directly, and will remain lost all their lives. Secondly, there are those who have enough sense or modesty to realize that they are ⌐less wise ⌐and⌐ less able to distinguish the true from the false⌐ than are others, and so should rather be satisfied to follow the opinions of these others than to search for better ones themselves. [16]

As for myself, I should no doubt have belonged in the last class if I had had but a single teacher or if I had not known the differences which have always existed among the most learned. I had discovered in college that one cannot imagine anything so strange and unbelievable but that it has been upheld by some philosopher; and in my travels I had found that those who held opinions contrary to ours were neither barbarians nor savages, but that many of them were at least as reasonable as ourselves. I had considered how the same man, with the same capacity for reason, becomes different as a result of being brought up among Frenchmen or Germans than he would be if he had been brought up among Chinese or ⌐Americans ⌐or⌐ cannibals⌐; and how, in our fashions, the thing which pleased us ten years ago and perhaps will please us again ten years in the future, now seems extravagant and ridiculous; (549) and felt that in all these ways we are much more greatly influenced by custom and example than by any certain knowledge. Faced with this divergence of opinion, I could not accept the testimony of the majority, for I thought it worthless as a proof of anything somewhat difficult to discover, since it is much more likely that a single man will have discovered it than a whole people. Nor, on the other hand, could I select anyone whose opinions seemed to me to be preferable to those of others, and I was thus constrained to embark on the investigation for myself.

Nevertheless, like a man who walks alone in the darkness, I resolved to go so slowly and [17] circumspectly that if I did not get ahead very rapidly I was at least safe from falling. Also, ⌐just as the occupants of an old house do not destroy it before a plan for a new one has been thought out,⌐ I did not want to reject all the opinions which had slipped irrationally into my consciousness since birth, until I had first spent enough time planning how to accomplish the task which I was then undertaking, and seeking the true method of obtaining knowledge of everything which my mind was capable of understanding.

Among the branches of philosophy, I had, when younger, studied logic, and among those of mathematics, geometrical analysis and algebra; three arts or sciences which should have been able to contribute something to my design. But in examining them I noticed that as far as logic was concerned, its syllogisms and most of its other methods serve rather to explain to another what one already knows, or even, as in the art of Lully, to speak ⌐freely and⌐ without judgment of what one does not know, than to learn new things. Although it does contain many true and good precepts, they are interspersed among so many others that are harmful or superfluous that it is almost as difficult to separate them as to bring forth a Diana or a Minerva from a block of virgin marble. Then, as far as the analysis of the Greeks and the algebra of the moderns is concerned, besides the fact that they deal with ⌐abstractions and⌐ ⌐speculations which⌐ appear to have no utility, the first is always so limited to the consideration of figures that it cannot exercise the [18] understanding without greatly fatiguing the imagination, and the last is so limited to certain rules and certain numbers that it has become a confused and obscure art which perplexes the mind instead of a science which educates it. In consequence I thought that some other method must be found (550) to combine the advantages of these three and to escape their faults. Finally, just as the multitude of laws frequently furnishes an excuse for vice, and a state is much better governed with a few laws which are strictly adhered to, so I thought that instead of the great number of precepts of which logic is composed, I would have enough with the four following ones, provided that I made a firm and unalterable resolution not to violate them even in a single instance.

The first rule was never to accept anything as true unless I recognized it to be ⌐certainly and⌐ evidently such: that is, carefully to avoid ⌐all⌐ precipitation and prejudgment, and to include nothing in my conclusions unless it presented itself so clearly and distinctly to my mind that there was no ⌐reason for⌐ occasion⌐ to doubt it.

The second was to divide each of the difficulties which I encountered into as many parts as possible, and as might be required for an easier solution.

The third was to think in an orderly fashion ⌐when concerned with the search for truth⌐, beginning with the things which were simplest and easiest to understand, and gradually and by degrees reaching toward more complex knowledge, even treating, as though ordered, [19] materials which were not necessarily so.

The last was ⌐, both in the process of searching and in reviewing when in difficulty,⌐ always to make enumerations so complete, and reviews so general, that I would be certain that nothing was omitted.

Those long chains of reasoning, so simple and easy, which enabled the geometricians to reach the most difficult demonstrations, had made me wonder whether all things knowable to men might not fall into a similar logical sequence. If so, we need only refrain from accepting as true that which is not

true, and carefully follow the order necessary to deduce each
one from the others, and there cannot be any propositions so
abstruse that we cannot prove them, or so recondite that we
cannot discover them. It was not very difficult, either, to decide where we should look for a beginning, for I knew already that one begins with the simplest and easiest to know.
Considering that among all those who have previously sought
truth in the sciences, mathematicians alone have been able to
find some demonstrations, some certain and evident reasons,
I had no doubt that I should begin where they did, although
I expected no advantage (551) except to accustom my mind to
work with truths and not to be satisfied with bad reasoning. I
do not mean that I intended to learn all the particular
branches of mathematics; for [20] I saw that although the objects they discuss are different, all these branches are in agreement in limiting their consideration to the relationships or
proportions between their various objects. I judged therefore
that it would be better to examine these proportions in general, and use particular objects as illustrations only in order to
make their principles easier to comprehend, and to be able
the more easily to apply them afterwards, without any forcing,
to anything for which they would be suitable. I realized that
in order to understand the principles of relationships I would
sometimes have to consider them singly, and sometimes ⟨com-
prehend and remember them⟩ in groups. I thought I could
consider them better singly as relationships between lines, because I could find nothing more simple or more easily pictured to my imagination and my senses. But in order to remember and understand them better when taken in groups, I
had to express them in numbers, and in the smallest numbers
possible. Thus I took the best traits of geometrical analysis
and algebra, and corrected the faults of one by the other.

The exact observation of the few precepts which I had
chosen gave me such facility in clarifying all the issues in these
two sciences that it took only two or three months to examine
them. I began with the most simple and general, and each
truth that I found was a rule which [21] helped me to find

others, so that I not only solved many problems which I had previously judged very difficult, but also it seemed to me that toward the end I could determine to what extent a still unsolved problem could be solved, and what procedures should be used in solving it. In this I trust that I shall not appear too vain, considering that there is only one true solution to a given problem, and whoever finds it knows all that anyone can know about it. Thus, for example, a child who has learned arithmetic and performed an addition according to the rules may feel certain that, as far as that particular sum is concerned, he has found everything that a human mind can discover. For, after all, the method of (552) following the correct order and stating precisely all the circumstances of what we are investigating is the whole of what gives certainty to the rules of arithmetic.

What pleased me most about this method was that it enabled me to reason in all things, if not perfectly, at least as well as was in my power. In addition, I felt that in practicing it my mind was gradually ⟨dissipating its uncertainties and⟩ becoming accustomed to conceive its objects more clearly and distinctly, and since I had not directed this method to any particular subject matter, I was in hopes of applying it just as usefully to the difficulties of other sciences as I had already to those of ⟨geometry or⟩ algebra. Not that I would dare to undertake to examine at once all the difficulties that presented themselves, for that would have been contrary to the principle of order. But I had observed that all the basic principles of the sciences were taken from [22] philosophy, which itself had no certain ones. It therefore seemed that I should first attempt to establish philosophic principles, and that since this was the most important thing in the world and the place where precipitation and prejudgment were most to be feared, I should not attempt to reach conclusions until I had attained a much more mature age than my then twenty-three years, and had spent much time in preparing for it. This preparation would consist partly in freeing my mind from the false opinions which I had previously acquired, partly in building up a fund of experiences which should serve afterwards as the raw material of my reasoning, and partly in training myself in the method which I had determined upon, so that I should become more and more adept in its use.

PART THREE

SOME MORAL RULES DERIVED FROM THE METHOD

In planning to rebuild one's house it is not enough to draw up the plans for the new dwelling, tear down the old one, and provide ⟨stones and other⟩ materials ⟨useful for building,⟩ and obtain workmen for the task. We must see that we are provided with a comfortable place to stay while the work of rebuilding is going on. Similarly in my own case; while reason obliged me to be irresolute in my beliefs, there was no reason why I should be so in my actions. In order to live as happily as possible during the interval I prepared a provisional code of morality for myself, consisting of three or four maxims which I here set forth.

The first was to obey the laws and [23] customs of my country, constantly retaining the religion ⟨which I judged best, and⟩ in which, by God's grace, I had been brought up since childhood, and in all other matters to follow the most (553) moderate and least excessive opinions to be found in the practices of the more judicious part of the community in which I would live. For I was then about to discard my own opinions in order to re-examine them, and meanwhile could do no better than to follow those of the most reliable judges. While there may be, no doubt, just as reliable persons among the Persians or the Chinese as among ourselves, it seemed more practical to pattern my conduct on that of the society in which I would have to live. Furthermore, it seemed to me that to learn people's true opinions, I should pay attention to their

conduct rather than to their words, not only because in our
corrupt times there are few who are ready to say all that they
believe, but also because many are not aware of their own
beliefs, since the mental process of knowing a thing is ⟨good
or bad is⟩ distinct from, and can occur without, the mental
process of knowing that we know it. Among a number of
opinions equally widely accepted, I chose only the most moderate, partly because these are always the most convenient in
practice and, since excess is usually bad, presumably the best;
but also so that I should stray a shorter distance from the true
road in case I should make a mistake, than I would in choosing one extreme when it was the other that should have been
followed. In particular, [24] I considered as ⟨extreme or⟩ excessive all the promises by which we abandon some of our
freedom. Not that I disapproved of the laws which, to remedy
the inconstancy of vacillating spirits, permit them to make
bonds or contracts which oblige them to persevere with their
intentions, provided the intentions are good, or at least not
bad, but because I recognized that nothing is unchanging,
and that in my own case I was proposing to improve my judgment more and more, not to make it worse. It would therefore
have been a major violation of common sense if I obliged myself to continue to accept a thing I formerly approved after it
ceased to merit approval, or after I altered my opinion of it.

My second maxim was to be as firm and determined in my
actions as I could be, and not to act on the most doubtful decisions, once I had made them, any less resolutely than on the
most certain. In this matter I patterned my behavior on that
of travelers, who, finding themselves lost in a forest, must not
wander about, (554) now turning this way, now that, and still
less should remain in one place, but should go as straight as
they can in the direction they first select and not change the
direction except for the strongest reasons. By this method,
even if the direction was chosen at random, they will presumably arrive [25] at some destination, not perhaps where
they would like to be, but at least where they will be better
off than in the middle of the forest. Similarly, situations in life

often permit no delay; and when we cannot determine the course which is certainly best, we must follow the one which is probably the best; and when we cannot determine even that, we must nevertheless select one and follow it thereafter as though it were certainly best. If the course selected is not indeed a good one, at least the reasons for selecting it are excellent. This frame of mind freed me also from the repentance and remorse commonly felt by those vacillating individuals who are always seeking as worth while things which they later judge to be bad.

My third maxim was always to seek to conquer myself rather than fortune, to change my desires rather than the established order, and generally to believe that nothing except our thoughts is wholly under our control, so that after we have done our best in external matters, what remains to be done is absolutely impossible, at least as far as we are concerned. This maxim in itself should suffice to prevent me from desiring in the future anything which I could not acquire, and thus to make me happy. For it is our nature to [26] desire only that which we imagine to be somehow attainable, and if we consider all external benefits equally beyond our reach we will no more regret being unjustly deprived of our birthright than we regret not possessing the kingdoms of China or Mexico. Thus, making a virtue of necessity, we no more desire to be well when we are sick, or to be free when we are in prison, than we now desire bodies as incorruptible as diamonds, or wings to fly like the birds. (555) But I must admit that it takes much practice and frequently repeated meditations to become accustomed to view things in this manner, and I think that this must have been the principal secret of those philosophers of ancient times who were able to rise above fortune, and, despite pains and poverty, to vie with the gods in happiness. Being constantly occupied in considering the limits imposed upon them by nature, they were so perfectly convinced that nothing was really theirs but their thoughts that that alone was sufficient to keep them from any concern in other things. Their control of their thoughts, on the other hand, was so absolute ⟨, that is, they were so accustomed to regulate their desires and other passions,⟩ that they had some justification for considering themselves richer and more powerful, more free and happier, than any other man who did not have this philosophy, and who, however [27] much he might be favored by nature and fortune, had no such control over his desires.

Finally, I planned to make a review of the various occupations possible in this life, in order to choose the best. Without intending to disparage other occupations, I thought I could do no better than to continue in the one I was engaged in, employing my life in improving my mind and increasing as far as I could my knowledge of the truth by following the method that I had outlined for myself. I had experienced such periods of great happiness after I had begun to use this method, that I could hope for no greater or more innocent joys in this life. In discovering day after day truths which seemed fairly important and generally unknown to other men, I was filled with such satisfaction that other considerations did not affect me. Another reason for my decision was that the three maxims previously considered were based on my plan to continue the search for truth. For as God has given each one of us some ability to distinguish the true from the false, I should not have been content for one instant to rely on the opinions of others if I had not planned to use my own judgment at the proper time; nor could I have followed those opinions with a clear conscience if I had not hoped to take advantage of every opportunity to find better ones, if better ones [28] there were. And finally, I could not have limited my desires, nor been happy ⟨with the things within my power⟩, if I were not following a path by which I expected to obtain all the knowledge of which I was capable (556) and, by the same token, all the real values to which I might aspire. Besides, since our will neither seeks nor avoids anything except as it is judged good or bad by our reason, good judgment is sufficient to guarantee good behavior. Judging as best one can therefore implies that one acts as well as one can, or in other words, that one will acquire all the virtues and with them all other possible goods.

Once we are sure of this, we cannot well fail to be happy ⌐and blesscd⌐.

After thus assuring myself of these maxims, and having put them aside with the truths of the Faith, which have always been most certain to me, I judged that I could proceed freely to reject all my other beliefs. And inasmuch as I hoped to obtain my end more readily by conversing with men than by remaining any longer ⌐alone⌐ in my ⌐warm⌐ retreat, ⌐where I had had all these thoughts,⌐ I proceeded on my way before winter was wholly passed. In the nine years that followed I wandered here and there throughout the world, trying everywhere to be spectator rather than actor in all the comedies that go on. I took particular pains in judging each thing to seek out whatever elements of uncertainty it contained, which might cause us to conceive false opinions about it. Meanwhile I tried to clear my mind of all the errors that had [29] previously accumulated. In this I did not wish to imitate the sceptics, who doubted only for the sake of doubting and intended to remain always irresolute; on the contrary, my whole purpose was to achieve greater certainty and to reject the loose earth and sand in favor of rock and clay. In all these things I seemed to succeed well enough, for, as I was trying to discover the falsity or uncertainty of the propositions I was examining, not by feeble conjectures but by clear and assured reasonings, I encountered nothing that did not lead me to some certain conclusions, even if it were only that the matter was wholly uncertain. And just as in tearing down a building we usually retain the debris to help build a new one, so in destroying all of my opinions which seemed to me ill-founded, I made many observations and acquired much experience which has since aided me in establishing more certain knowledge. In addition, I continued to practice the method which I had decided upon; and besides conducting all my thoughts according to its rules, I set aside a few hours now and then for practice upon mathematical difficulties. In some cases I even practiced upon some other difficulties (557) which could be made to parallel mathematical ones by rejecting those principles of the sciences in question

which I did not find sufficiently well established, as I have
explained in some of my other writings. Thus I lived, in [30]
appearance, just like those who have nothing to do but to live
a pleasant and innocent life and attempt to obtain the pleas-
ures without the vices, to enjoy their leisure without ennui,
and to occupy their time with all the respectable amusements
available. But in reality I never desisted from my design and
continued to achieve greater acquaintance with truth, perhaps more than I would have if I had only read books or
sought the society of men of letters.

In any case, nine years passed before I reached my decision
about the difficulties ordinarily in dispute among the learned,
and before I sought to lay the groundwork of a philosophy
more certain than popular belief. The example of several men
of excellent abilities who had previously attempted my task
and who, in my opinion, had failed, made me fear so many
difficulties that I should perhaps not have dared to start so
soon if I had not learned of a rumor that I had already completed my philosophy. I did not know on what such an opinion was based; if I contributed somewhat to it by my conversation, it must have been by confessing my ignorance more
freely than is usually the case among those who have studied
a little, and possibly also by presenting my reasons for doubting many things that others deemed certain. I am sure that I
did not boast of any doctrines. But I did not want to be taken
for more than I was, and so I thought that I should try by
all means to make myself worthy of [31] my reputation. Just
eight years ago, therefore, I decided to abandon those places
where I would be among acquaintances, and retired to Hol-
land, where the long duration of the war produced such conditions that the armies billeted there seemed but to guarantee
the fruits of peace. There, in the midst of a great and busy
people, more interested in their own affairs than curious about
those of others, I was able to enjoy all the comforts of life to
be found in the most populous cities while living in as solitary
and retired a fashion as though in the most remote of deserts.

PART FOUR

PROOFS OF THE EXISTENCE OF GOD
AND OF THE HUMAN SOUL

I do not know whether I ought to touch upon my first meditations here, for they are so metaphysical and out (558) of the ordinary that they might not be interesting to most people. Nevertheless, in order to show whether my fundamental notions are sufficiently sound, I find myself more or less constrained to speak of them. I had noticed for a long time that in practice it is sometimes necessary to follow opinions which we know to be very uncertain, just as though they were indubitable, as I stated before; but inasmuch as I desired to devote myself wholly to the search for truth, I thought that I should take a course precisely contrary, and reject as absolutely false anything of which I could have the least doubt, in order to see whether anything would be left after this procedure which could be called wholly certain. Thus, [32] as our senses deceive us at times, I was ready to suppose that nothing was at all the way our senses represented them to be. As there are men who make mistakes in reasoning even on the simplest topics in geometry, I judged that I was as liable to error as any other, and rejected as false all the reasoning which I had previously accepted as valid demonstration. Finally, as the same percepts which we have when awake may come to us when asleep without their being true, I decided to suppose that nothing that had ever entered my mind was more real than the illusions of my dreams. But I soon noticed that while I thus wished to think everything false, it was necessarily true that I who thought so was something. Since this truth, *I think, therefore I am,* ⟨or exist,⟩ was so firm and assured that all the most extravagant suppositions of the sceptics were unable to shake it, I judged that I could safely accept it as the first principle of the philosophy I was seeking.

I then examined closely what I was, and saw that I could imagine that I had no body, and that there was no world nor any place that I occupied, but that I could not imagine for a moment that I did not exist. On the contrary, from the very fact that I doubted the truth of other things, ⟨or had any other thought,⟩ it followed ⌈very⌉ evidently ⌈and very certainly⌉ that I existed. On the other hand, if I had [33] ceased to think while ⟨my body and the world and⟩ all the rest of what I had ever imagined remained true, I would have had no reason to believe that I existed ⟨during that time⟩; therefore I concluded that I was a ⟨thing or⟩ substance whose whole essence or nature was only to think, and which, to exist, has no need of space nor of any material thing ⟨or body⟩. Thus it follows that this ego, ⟨this mind,⟩ ⌈this soul,⌉ by which I am what I am, (559) is entirely distinct from the body and is easier to know than the latter, and that even if the body were not, the soul would not cease to be all that it now is.

Next, I considered in general what is required of a proposition for it to be true and certain, for since I had just discovered one to be such, I thought I ought also to know of what that certitude consisted. I saw that there was nothing at all in this statement, "I think, therefore I am," to assure me that I was saying the truth, unless it was that I saw very clearly that to think one must exist. So I judged that I could accept as a general rule that the things which we conceive very clearly and ⌈very⌉ distinctly are always true, but that there may well be some difficulty in deciding which are those which we conceive distinctly.

After that I reflected ⌈upon the fact⌉ that I doubted ⟨many things⟩, and that, in consequence, my spirit was not wholly perfect, for I saw clearly that it was a greater perfection to know than to doubt. I decided to ascertain from what source I had learned to think of something more perfect than myself, and it appeared evident that it must have been [34] from some nature which was in fact more perfect. As for my ideas about many other things outside of me, as the sky, earth, light, heat, and thousands of other things, I was not so much troubled to discover where they came from, because I found nothing in them superior to my own nature. If they really existed, I could believe that whatever perfection they possessed might be derived from my own nature; if they did not exist, I could believe that they were derived from nothingness, that is, that they were derived from my own defects. But this could not be the explanation of my ⟨thought or⟩ idea of a being more perfect than my own. To derive it from nothingness was manifestly impossible, and it is no less repugnant to good sense to assume what is more perfect comes from and depends on the less perfect than it is to assume that something comes from nothing, so that I could not assume that it came from myself. Thus the only hypothesis left was that this idea was put in my mind by a nature that was really more perfect than I was, which had all the perfections that I could imagine, and which was, in a word, God. To this I added that since I knew some perfections which I did not possess, I was not the only being in existence—I will here use freely, if you will pardon me, the terms of the school—and that it followed of necessity that there was someone else more perfect upon whom I depended and from whom I had acquired all that I possessed. For if I had been alone and independent of anything else, so that I had (560) bestowed [35] upon myself all that limited quantity of value which I shared with the perfect Being, I would have been able to get from myself, in the same way, all the surplus which I recognize as lacking in me, and so would have been myself infinite, eternal, immutable, omniscient, omnipotent, and, in sum, I would possess all the perfections that I could discover in God.

For to know the nature of God, ⟨whose existence has been proved⟩, following the reasoning which I have just explained, as far as I was capable of such knowledge, I had only to consider each quality of which I had an idea, and decide whether it was or was not a perfection to possess that quality. I would then be certain that none of those which had some imperfection were in him, but that all the others were. I saw that doubt, inconstancy, sorrow and similar things could not be part of

God's nature, since I would be happy to be without them myself. In addition, I had ideas of many sensible and corporeal
entities, for although I might suppose that I was dreaming and
that all that I saw or imagined was false, I could not at any
rate deny that the ideas were truly in my consciousness. ⌐Since⌐
I had already recognized very clearly that intelligent nature is
distinct from corporeal nature ⌐, and that in every composite
one part depended upon another, and the whole upon its
parts, and that whatever depends upon something else is not
perfect⌐ ⌐, I considered that composition is an evidence of dependency and that dependency is manifestly a defect⌐. From
this I judged that it could not be a perfection in God to be
composed of these two natures, and that consequently he was
not so composed. But if there were in the world bodies, or
even intelligences or other natures that were not wholly [36]
perfect, their being must depend on God's power in such a
way that they could not subsist without him for a single moment.

At this point I wished to seek for other truths, and proposed
for consideration the object of the geometricians. This I conceived as a continuous body, or a space infinitely extended in
length, breadth, and ⌐height or⌐ depth; divisible into various
parts which can have different shapes and sizes and can be
moved or transposed in any way: all of which is presumed by
geometricians to be true of their object. I went through some
of their simplest demonstrations and noticed that the great
certainty which everyone attributes to them is only based on
the fact that they are ⌐clearly and⌐ evidently conceived, following the rule previously established. I noticed also that there
was nothing at all in them to assure me of the existence of
their object; it was clear, for example, that if we posit a triangle, its three angles must be (561) equal to two right angles,
but there was nothing in that to assure me that there was a
single triangle in the world. When I turned back to my idea
of a perfect Being, on the other hand, I ⌐immediately⌐ discovered that existence was included in that idea in the same
way that the idea of a triangle contains the equality of its

angles to two right angles, or that the idea of a ⌈sphere ⌐or⌉ circle⌐ includes the equidistance of all its parts from its center. Perhaps, in fact, the existence of the perfect Being is even more evident. Consequently, it is at least as certain that God, who is this perfect Being, exists, as any theorem of geometry could possibly be. [37]

What makes many people feel that it is difficult to know of the existence of God, or even of the nature of their own souls, is that they never ⌐withdraw their minds from their senses and⌐ consider things higher than corporeal objects. They are so accustomed never to think of anything without picturing it ⌐, that is, without picturing in their imagination some image, as though of a corporeal thing,⌐ ⌈—a method of thinking suitable only for material objects—⌉ that everything which is not picturable seems to them unintelligible. This is also manifest in the fact that even philosophers hold it as a maxim in the schools that there is nothing in the understanding which was not first in the senses, a location where it is clearly evident that the ideas of God and of the soul have never been. It seems to me that those who wish to use imagery to understand these matters are doing precisely the same thing that they would be doing if they tried to use their eyes to hear sounds or smell odors. There is even this difference: that the sense of sight gives us no less certainty of the truth of objects than do those of smell and hearing, while neither our imagery nor our senses could assure us of anything without the co-operation of our understanding ⌐or reason⌐.

Finally, if there are still some men who are not sufficiently persuaded of the existence of God and of their souls ⌐as really existing things considered apart from the body,⌐ by the reasons which I have given, I want them to understand that all the other things of which they might think themselves more certain, such as their having a body, or the existence of stars and of an earth, and other such things are less certain. For even though we have a moral assurance ⌐, as philosophers say,⌐ of these things, such that it seems [38] we cannot doubt them without extravagance, yet without being unreasonable we cannot deny that, as far as metaphysical certainty goes, there is sufficient room for doubt. For we can imagine, when asleep, that we have another body and see other stars and another earth without there being any such. How could one know that the thoughts which come to us in dreams are false rather than the others ⸤which we have when awake⸥, since they are often no less vivid and detailed? (562) Let the best minds study this question as long as they wish, I do not believe they can find any reason good enough to remove this doubt unless they presuppose the existence of God. The very principle which I took as a rule to start with, namely, that all those things which we conceived very clearly and very distinctly are true, is known to be true only because God exists, and because he is a ⸤supreme and⸥ perfect Being, and because everything in us ⸤necessarily⸥ comes from him. From this it follows that our ideas or notions, being real things which come from God insofar as they are clear and distinct, cannot to that extent fail to be true. Consequently, though we often have ideas which contain falsity, they can only be those ideas which contain some confusions and obscurity, in which respect they ⸤do not come from the supreme Being, but proceed from ⸤or⸥ participate in⸥ nothingness. That is to say, they are ⸤obscure and⸥ confused in us only because we ⸤lack something or⸥ are not wholly perfect. It is evident that it is no less ⸤impossible ⸤and⸥ repugnant to good sense⸥ to assume that falsity or [39] imperfection as such is derived from God, as that truth or perfection is derived from nothingness. But if we did not know that all reality and truth within us came from a perfect and infinite Being, however clear and distinct our ideas might be, we would have no reason to be certain that they were ⸤endowed with the perfection of being⸥ true.

After the knowledge of God and the soul has thus made us certain of our rule, it is easy to see that the ⸤errors of our⸥ dreams ⸤which we have when asleep⸥ do not in any way cast doubt upon the truth of our waking thoughts. For if it happened that we had some very distinct idea, even while sleeping, as for example when a geometrician dreams of some new proof, his sleep does not keep the proof from being good. As for the most common error of dreams, which is to picture various objects in the same way as our external senses represent them to us ᐟwhen awakeᐟ, it does not matter if this gives us a reason to distrust the truth of the impressions we receive ᐟ, or think we receive,ᐟ from the senses, because we can also be mistaken in them frequently without being asleep, as when jaundiced persons see everything yellow, or as the stars and other distant objects appear much smaller than they really are. For in truth, whether we are asleep or awake, we should never allow ourselves to be convinced except on the evidence of our reason. Note that I say of our *reason,* and not of our imagination or of our senses; for even though we see the [40] sun very clearly, we must not judge thereby that its size is such as we see it, and we can well imagine distinctly the head of a lion (563) mounted on the body of a goat, without concluding that a chimera exists in this world. For reason does not insist that all we see or visualize in this way is true, but it does insist that all our ideas or notions must have some foundation in truth, for it would not be possible that God, who is all-perfect and wholly truthful, would otherwise have given them to us. Since our reasonings ᐟor judgmentsᐟ are never as ᐟclear and distinct ᒥ, asᐟ evident or as completeᒥ in sleep as in waking life, although sometimes our imaginations are then ᒥasᒥ lively and detailed ᒥas when awake, or even more soᒥ, and since reason tells us also that all our thoughts cannot be true, as we are not wholly perfect; whatever of truth is to be found in our ideas will ᒥinevitablyᒥ occur in those which we have when awake rather than in our dreams.

PART FIVE

SOME QUESTIONS OF PHYSICS

I would have been glad to continue my exposition and exhibit here the whole chain of other truths which I deduced from these basic ones, but for the fact that to do so I should have to speak of many questions which are in dispute among the learned. As I do not wish to embroil myself with them, I think it would be better to abstain, so I shall give only an outline of these views, and let wiser people judge whether the public should be informed in greater detail.

I have [41] always remained true to the resolution I made, never to suppose any other principle than that which I have just used to demonstrate the existence of God and the soul, and not to admit anything as true which did not seem to me clearer and more certain than the demonstrations of the geometricians previously seemed. Nevertheless, I have not only succeeded in satisfying myself in this short time on all the principal difficulties usually treated in philosophy, but have also discovered certain laws which God has so established in nature, and the notion of which he has so fixed in our minds, that after sufficient reflection we cannot doubt that they are exactly observed in all which exists or which happens in the world. Finally, in considering the implications of these laws I seem to have discovered several truths ⌈more useful and⌉ more important than anything I had previously learned or even hoped to learn.

Since I have tried to explain the most important of these laws in a work which certain considerations prevent my publishing, I see no better way to proceed than by summarizing its contents. I intended to include in it all that I thought I knew, before writing it, concerning the nature of material things. But I found myself in the same state as painters, who cannot equally well represent in a two-dimensional painting all the various faces of a solid body, and so choose one to bring to the light, and leave the others in shadow, [42] so that (564) they can be seen only while viewing the selected side. Therefore, fearing that I would not be able to put into any discourse all that I intended, I undertook solely to describe at length what I thought on the subject of light, and took that occasion to add something concerning the sun and the fixed stars, since they are almost the only sources of light; of the sky, since it transmits it; of the planets, the comets, and the earth, since they reflect it; and in particular of all the objects on earth, since they are either colored or transparent or luminous; and finally of man, since he is the observer of it. I even elected, as a painter might do, to place my object somewhat in the shadow, so that I could express my opinions more freely without being obliged to accept or to refute the opinions commonly held by the learned. I therefore resolved to leave this world for them to dispute about, and to speak only of what would happen in a new one, if God should now create, somewhere in imaginary space, enough matter to make one; and if he agitated the various parts of this matter without order, making a chaos as confused as the poets could imagine, but that afterward he did nothing but lend his usual support to nature, allowing it to behave according to the laws he had established.

So I first described this matter and tried to picture it in such a way that nothing in the world could be clearer or more intelligible except what has just been said about God and the soul. I even expressly supposed that this matter [43] had none of the forms or qualities concerning which one disputes in the schools, nor in general anything that we do not know so naturally that we cannot even pretend to ignore it. Furthermore, I showed what were the laws of nature, and without basing my reasons on anything more specific than the infinite perfection⌈s⌉ of God, I tried to demonstrate everything which might be doubtful, and to show that nature is such that even if God had created several worlds, there would have been none where these laws were not observed. After that, I showed how the greater part of the matter in this chaos would, in consequence of these laws, become arranged in a manner which would make it similar to our skies; and how nevertheless some of the parts must compose an earth, and some planets and comets, and others a sun and fixed stars. And here, enlarging upon the topic of light, I explained at considerable length its nature when contained in the sun and the stars, how from there it traverses in an instant the immense reaches of the heavens, and how it is reflected from the planets and comets toward the earth. I also added several things concerning the substance, situation, movements, and all the diverse qualities of these celestial objects and stars; (565) until I thought I had said enough to show that there were no phenomena ⟨in the sky or stars⟩ of this world which would not or at least could not occur similarly in the world [44] I was describing.

Thence I went on to speak particularly of the earth: how, even though I had expressly supposed that God had given no weight to the matter of which it was composed, all its parts would tend exactly toward its center; how the disposition of the celestial bodies and stars, principally the moon, would cause an ebb and flow in the water and air on its surface, similar in all respects to the tides of our seas, and in addition a certain current, as much of water as of air, from east to west, such as we find in the tropics; how mountains, seas, springs and rivers could naturally occur, metals come to be in mines, plants grow in the fields, and, in general, how the whole genus of mixed or composite objects would be formed.

Among other things, since outside of the stars I knew nothing but fire which produced light, I strove to explain quite clearly the whole of the nature of fire: how it is produced and maintained; how sometimes it has heat without light and sometimes light without heat; how it can produce different colors in different objects, and many other qualities; how it melts some objects and hardens others; how it can consume things entirely or convert them into ashes and smoke; and finally, how by the violence of its action it turns ashes into glass; for as this transmutation of [45] ashes into glass seemed as admirable as any that occurs in nature, I found a particular pleasure in describing it.

I did not wish to infer from all this that the world had been created in the manner I proposed, for it is much more likely that God created it in the beginning in the form it was to assume. But it is certain, and this is an opinion commonly held by theologians, that the action by which the world is now conserved is precisely the same as that by which it was created. Even therefore, if God had given the world in the beginning no other form but chaos, and had only established the laws of nature and given his concurrence for the world to behave as it usually does, one can believe, without injustice to the miracle of creation, that all material objects could have become, in time, such as we see them at present. Their nature is much easier to conceive when one pictures their gradual growth in this manner rather than considering them as produced in their completed state.

From the description of inanimate objects and plants I passed (566) to ⌈that of⌉ animals, and particularly ⌈of⌉ man. But I did not as yet know enough to speak of these in the same style as of the rest, in showing the causes of their existence and showing from what origins and in what manner nature must have produced them. I was therefore satisfied to assume that God formed the body of a man just like [46] our own, both in the external configuration of its members and in the internal configuration of its organs, without using in its composition any matter but that which I had described. I also assumed that God did not put into this body, to start with, any rational soul or any other entity to serve as a vegetable or sensitive soul, beyond kindling in the heart one of those fires without light which I had already described and which I considered to be entirely similar to that which heats grain when it is stored before it is dry, or which warms new wines when they are allowed to ferment before being separated from the grapes. Examining the functions which such a body would have, I discovered everything that can exist without thinking; everything except that which is contributed by the soul: that part of us distinct from the body whose essence, as we have previously said, is only to think. These functions are the same as those in which the unreasoning animals resemble us, and do not include any of those which are dependent on thinking and which belong to us as men. These human qualities I discovered somewhat later, when I supposed that God created a rational soul and joined it to the body in a certain fashion which I described.

In order to show how I treated this matter, I wish to insert here the explanation of the function of the heart and arteries. As the first and most general function found in animals, it will serve to indicate what the reader should [47] think of all the rest. Those who are not well versed in anatomy will find less difficulty in understanding what I am going to say if they will take the trouble, before reading this, to have the heart of some large animal cut open before them, for the heart of an animal with lungs is quite similar to that of man. Let them then observe the two chambers, or ventricles, which it contains. First, the one on the right side connects with two very large tubes: the *vena cava,* which is the principal container of blood and resembles the trunk of a tree of which all the other veins are branches; and the *vena arteriosa,* misnamed since it is really an artery which starts in the heart, then divides into several branches, and spreads throughout the lungs. The left ventricle has two similar tubes at least as large as those just described: (567) the *arteria venosa,* likewise misnamed since it is purely a vein, coming from the lungs, where it is divided into a number of branches interlaced with those of the *vena arteriosa* and those of the windpipe, through which enters the air we breathe; and the aorta, which, starting from the heart, sends its branches everywhere throughout the body. I should suggest also that the reader observe the eleven little membranes which, like so many little valves, open and close the four openings in these two ventricles. [48] Three are at the entrance to the *vena cava,* where they are so disposed that they cannot stop the blood that it contains from flowing into the right ventricle but prevent any of it from flowing back. Three, at the entrance of the *vena arteriosa,* are disposed in precisely the opposite fashion, permitting the blood in the heart to pass to the lungs but not allowing the blood in the lungs to return. So also, there are two at the entrance to the *arteria venosa,* which permit the blood to pass from the lungs to the left ventricle and prevent its return, and three at the entrance to the aorta, permitting the blood to leave the heart but not to return. There is no need to seek any other reason for the number of these membranes other than the fact that the opening of the *arteria venosa,* being oval because of its location, can be conveniently closed with two, while the others are round and can be more readily closed with three. I should like the reader to notice also that the aorta and the *vena arteriosa* are much harder and firmer than the *arteria venosa* and *vena cava,* and that these last two are enlarged near the heart, forming two sacs called the "ears" or auricles of the heart, composed of a flesh resembling that of the ears. Notice also that there is always more heat in the heart than in any other part of the body, and that this heat is capable of causing any drop of blood which enters the ventricles to expand immediately, [49] just as any liquid does when it falls drop by drop into some very hot vessel.

After that, I need say nothing more to explain the functioning of the heart, except that when its ventricles are not full of blood, some necessarily flows into it. The right ventricle is filled from the *vena cava,* and the left ventricle from the *arteria venosa,* since these two vessels are always full and their entrances, opening toward the heart, cannot then be closed. The portions of blood in each ventricle cannot fail to be very large since the openings are very large and the vessels from which they came full of blood; and as soon as these portions enter the heart, they become rarefied and expand because of the heat there. This (568) dilates the whole heart and pushes upon and closes the five valvules at the entrance of the ⌈two⌉ vessels from which the blood comes, preventing any more blood from entering the heart. As the blood continues to expand, it pushes upon and opens the six other valvules which are at the entrance to the other two vessels through which the blood leaves, and thus inflates all the branches of the *vena arteriosa* and the aorta at almost the same instant as the heart. A moment later the heart and these arteries are all deflated because the blood which has entered them has cooled. The six valvules close, and the five of the *vena cava* and *arteria venosa* reopen permitting [50] two more portions of blood to enter and dilate the heart and the arteries the same as before. And since the blood which thus enters the heart comes through the two ⌈sacs called⌉ auricles, it follows that the condition of the latter is the opposite of that of the ventricles, and that the former are deflated when the latter are inflated.

For the rest, so that those who do not appreciate the force of mathematical demonstration and are not accustomed to distinguish between good and bad reasons should not make the mistake of denying this without examining it, I must warn them that the motion which I have just explained follows necessarily from the mere disposition of the parts of the heart visible to the naked eye, from the heat which one can feel with the fingers, and from the nature of the blood, which one can learn by experiment: just as the motions of a clock follow from the weight, location, and configuration of its counter-weights and wheels.

But if one asks why the blood in the veins does not become exhausted by thus flowing continually into the heart, and why the arteries do not become overfull, since all that passes through the heart goes there, I need only point out what has already been written by an English doctor [1] who has the glory of having broken the ice in this matter. He was the first to show that there are many small passages at the ends of the arteries, by which the blood received from the heart enters into the small branches of the veins, whence it returns again to the heart; so that its path is nothing but a [51] perpetual circulation. This he proved very adequately by the common experience of surgeons, who, having applied a tourniquet to

[1] [Harvey.]

the arm, not too tightly, above the spot where they open a vein, make the blood flow more abundantly than it would without the tourniquet. On the other hand, quite the contrary occurs if they tie it below, between the hand and the opening, or even if they tie it very tightly above. For it is obvious that a tourniquet which is moderately tight can prevent the blood which is already in the arm from returning toward the heart through the veins, but cannot hinder that which is continually coming from the heart through the arteries, because the arteries are situated below the veins, and because their walls are stiffer (569) and less easy to compress, and also because the blood comes from the heart with greater pressure than it has when returning through the veins. Since this blood leaves the arm through an opening in one of the veins, there must necessarily be some passages below the tourniquet, that is, toward the hand, by which it comes from the arteries. He also proves his contention about the circulation of the blood by certain small membranes 'in the form of valvules,' so disposed in various places along the veins that they do not permit the blood to flow from the middle of the body toward the extremities, but only to return from the extremities toward the heart; and further by the fact that all the blood in the body can be lost in a very short time when a single artery is cut, even if it is tightly constricted close to the heart and cut between the constriction and the heart, so that there [52] is no imaginable way that the blood which escapes comes from another source than the heart.

There are several other considerations which prove that the real cause of this movement of the blood is the one which I have given; such as, first, the difference between that which comes from the veins and that which comes from the arteries: a difference only to be explained by the fact that the blood is rarefied, as though it were distilled, in passing through the heart, and is therefore thinner, more active, and warmer when it has just come from there and is in the arteries, than just before it enters and is in the veins. Careful observation shows that this difference is more apparent near the heart, and is not

so noticeable at points far removed from it. Then the hardness of the membranes of which the *vena arteriosa* and the
aorta are composed shows well enough that the blood passes
through them with greater pressure than through the veins.
Furthermore, why should the left ventricle and the aorta be
larger and broader than the right ventricle and the *vena
arteriosa,* if it is not that the blood of the *arteria venosa,* not
having been in the lungs since it passed through the heart, is
thinner and becomes more rarefied more readily than that
which comes directly from the *vena cava*? And what could
doctors tell by feeling the pulse, if they did not know that as
the nature of the blood changes, it can be rarefied by the heat
of the heart more or less strongly and more or less rapidly
than before? And if we examine how this heat is communicated to the other parts of the body, must we not admit that it
is [53] through the blood which is warmed in passing through
the heart and spreads this heat through the whole body? From
this it results that if the blood is withdrawn from any part of
the body, heat is withdrawn by the same token. Even if the
heart were as hot as glowing iron, it could not warm the hands
and feet as it does unless it continually sent new blood to
those parts. We also recognize from these considerations that
the true purpose of respiration (570) is to bring enough fresh
air into the lungs to condense the blood which was rarefied
in the right ventricle before it returns to the left; to take
blood which has almost been converted into vapor and recon-
vert it into blood. If this were not done, the blood would not
be suitable for the nourishing of the heart's fire. This is confirmed by seeing that animals that have no lungs have only
one ventricle, and that unborn children, who cannot use their
lungs while enclosed in their mothers' wombs, have an opening through which blood flows directly from the *vena cava*
into the left ventricle, and a ⟨short⟩ tube by which it passes
from the *vena arteriosa* into the aorta without passing through
the lungs. Then, how could digestion take place in the
stomach if the heart did not send heat there through the
arteries, together with some of the most fluid parts of the

blood which help to dissolve the food which is placed there? Is it not easy to understand the action which converts the liquid part of these foods into blood if we consider that the blood is distilled possibly more than a hundred or two hundred times each day when passing through the heart? And we need say nothing more [54] to explain nutrition and the production of the several humors of the body, except that the force of the blood, expanding while passing from the heart to the ends of the arteries, brings it about that some of its parts come to rest in certain organs of the body, taking the place of others which they expel; and that certain parts of the blood come to rest in certain places rather than others, according to the location, shape, or size of the pores encountered; just as sieves with holes of different sizes serve to separate different grains from each other. The most remarkable aspect of all this is the production of animal spirits, which are like a very subtle wind, or rather a very pure ⌈and lively⌉ flame, which continuously rises in great abundance from the heart to the brain, and thence through the nerves into the muscles, where it produces the movement of all parts of the body. The most agitated and penetrating parts of the blood compose these animal spirits, and no other reason need be sought why these parts go to the brain rather than elsewhere than the fact that the arteries which conduct them are the straightest of all. According to the rules of mechanics, which are the same as the rules of nature, when several objects tend to move toward a place where there is not room enough for all, as is the case when parts of the blood leave the left ventricle and tend toward the brain, [55] the weakest and least agitated of them must ⌈necessarily⌉ be turned aside by the strongest, which thus are the only ones to arrive at their destination. (571)

I had explained all these things in sufficient detail in the treatise which I previously intended to publish. And I continued by showing what the nature of the network of nerves and muscles of the human body must be to enable the animal spirits within to move its members, as one sees when freshly severed heads still move and bite the earth although they are no longer alive. I showed what changes must take place in the brain to cause wakefulness, sleep, and dreams; how light, sounds, odors, tastes, heat, and all the other qualities of external objects can implant various ideas through the medium of the senses; and how hunger, thirst, and the other internal passions are communicated. I explained what must be understood by that animal sense which receives these ideas, by memory which retains them, and by imagination which can change them in various ways and build new ones from them, and thus, distributing the animal spirits in the muscles, move the parts of the body, in response to the objects, which are presented to the senses and the passions which are in the body, in as great a variety of ways as our own bodies can move without the guidance of volition. This will hardly seem strange to those who know how many ⌐motions can be produced in⌐ automata ⌐or machines ⌐which⌐ can be⌐ made by human industry, [56] although these automata employ very few ⌐wheels and other⌐ parts in comparison to the large number of bones, muscles, nerves, arteries, veins, and all the other component parts of each animal. Such persons will therefore think of this body as a machine created by the hand of God, and in consequence incomparably better designed and with more admirable movements than any machine that can be invented by man.

Here I paused to show that if there were any machines which had the organs and appearance of a monkey or of some other unreasoning animal, we would have no way of telling that it was not of the same nature as these animals. But if there were a machine which had such a resemblance to our bodies, and imitated our actions as far as is morally possible, there would always be two absolutely certain methods of recognizing that it was still not truly a man. The first is that it could never use words or other signs for the purpose of communicating its thoughts to others, as we do. It is indeed conceivable that a machine could be so made that it would utter words, and even words appropriate to ⌐the presence of⌐ ⌐physical acts ⌐or⌐ objects⌐ which cause some change in its organs; (572) as, for example, if it was touched in some spot that it would ask what you wanted to say to it; if in another, that it would cry that it was hurt, and so on for similar things. But it could never modify its phrases to [57] reply to the sense of whatever was said in its presence, as even the most stupid men can do. The second method of recognition is that, although such machines could do many things as well as, or perhaps even better than, men, they would infallibly fail in certain others, by which we would discover that they did not act by ⌜understanding ⌐or⌐ reason⌐, but only by the disposition of their organs. For while reason is a universal instrument which can be used in all sorts of situations, the organs have to be arranged in a particular way for each particular action. From this it follows that it is ⌜morally impossible ⌐and⌐ clearly incredible⌐ that there should be enough different devices in a machine to make it behave in all the occurrences of life as our reason makes us behave.

By these two methods we can also recognize the difference between man and animals. For it is a very remarkable thing that there are no men, not even the insane, so dull and stupid that they cannot put words together in a manner to convey their thoughts. On the contrary, there is no other animal, however perfect and fortunately situated it may be, that can do the same. And this is not because they lack the organs, for we see that magpies and parrots can pronounce words as well as we can, and nevertheless cannot speak as we do, that is, in showing that they think what they are saying. On the other hand, even those men born deaf and dumb, lacking the organs which others make use of in [58] speaking, and at least as badly off as the animals in this respect, usually invent for themselves some signs by which they make themselves understood by those who are with them enough to learn their language. And this proves not merely that animals have less reason than men, but that they have none at all, for we see that very little is needed in order to talk. Furthermore, we notice variations among animals of the same species, just as among men, and that some are easier to train than others.

It is therefore unbelievable that a monkey or a parrot which was one of the best of its species should not be the equal in this matter of one of the most stupid children, or at least of a child of infirm mind, if their soul were not of a wholly different nature from ours.

Note also that we should not confuse speech ⌐, and all those signs which in the practice of human beings convey thoughts,⌐ with the natural ⌐sounds and⌐ movements that indicate passions ⌐, and can be imitated by machines as well as by animals⌐; nor should we think, like some of the ancients, that animals speak although we (573) do not understand their language. For if it were true, they would make themselves understood by us as well as by their fellows, since they have several organs analogous to our own. It is another very remarkable fact that although there are many animals that show more industry than we in some of their behavior, these same animals show none at all in other ways; and so the fact that they do better than we do does not prove that they are rational, for on this basis they would be more rational than any of us, and [59] would surpass us in everything. It proves, on the contrary, that they are not rational, and that nature makes them behave as they do according to the disposition of their organs; just as a clock, composed only of wheels ⌐and weights⌐ ⌐and springs⌐, can count the hours and measure the time more accurately than we can with all our intelligence.

I then described the rational soul, and showed that it could not possibly be derived from the powers of matter, like the other things I have spoken about, but must have been specially created. I showed also that it would not suffice to place it in the human body, as a pilot in a ship, unless perhaps to move its parts, but that it must be more intimately joined and united with the body in order to have feelings and appetites like ours, and so constitute a real man. For the rest, I elaborated a little on the topic of the soul on account of its great importance; because, next to the error of those who deny God, which I think I have sufficiently refuted, there is none which is so apt to make weak characters stray from the path

of virtue as the idea that the souls of animals are of the same
nature as our own, and that in consequence we have no more
to fear or to hope for after this life than have the flies and
ants. Actually, when we know how different they are, we
understand more fully the reasons which prove that our soul
is by nature entirely independent of the body, and consequently does not have to die with it. Therefore, as long as
[60] we see no ⌐other⌐ causes which might destroy it, we are
naturally led to conclude that it is immortal.

PART SIX

SOME PREREQUISITES FOR FURTHER ADVANCES
IN THE STUDY OF NATURE

Three years ago, when I had completed the treatise containing all these matters, and when I was beginning to review
it for purposes of publication, I learned that people to whom
I defer, and whose authority over my actions is hardly less
than that of my own reason over my thoughts, had disapproved of a hypothesis in the field of physics that had been
published somewhat earlier by another person.[1] I do not want
to say that I had accepted that hypothesis, but at least before
their censure I could not imagine that it was prejudicial to religion or to the state, and therefore I could see no ground for
not professing it if reason (574) convinced me of its truth.
This circumstance made me fear that there might be other
opinions of mine in which I was misled, despite the great care
I had always taken not to accept any new ones which were not
very certainly demonstrated, and to write of none that might
prove disadvantageous to anyone. This occurrence was
enough to make me change my resolution to publish the
treatise, for although the reasons for making it were very

[1] [Galileo.]

strong, my inclinations were always much opposed to writing books and I was quick to find other reasons to excuse myself for not publishing. These reasons, on both sides, are such that not [61] only have I some interest in relating them, but the ⟨reading⟩ public may also have some interest in learning them.

I have never entertained any pretensions about the products of my thinking. When the result of the application of my methods was merely my own satisfaction concerning some speculative questions, or perhaps the regulation of my own behavior by the principles which it showed me, I did not feel obliged to write of them. For when it comes to morals, everyone is so convinced of his own good sense that there might be as many reformers as individuals if others than those whom God has established as sovereigns over his peoples, or to whom he has given enough grace and zeal to be prophets, were permitted to attempt reforms. So, even though my speculations pleased me very much, I believed that other persons had their own speculations which perhaps pleased them even more. As soon, however, as I had achieved some general notions about physics, and when, testing them in various critical problems, I noticed how far they might lead and how they differed from the principles accepted up to this time, I thought that I could not keep them hidden without gravely sinning against the rule that obliges us to promote as far as possible the general good of mankind. For they have satisfied me that it is possible to reach knowledge that will be of much utility in this life; and that instead of the speculative philosophy now taught in the schools we can find [62] a practical one, by which, knowing the nature and behavior of fire, water, air, stars, the heavens, and all the other bodies which surround us, as well as we now understand the different skills of our workers, we can employ these entities for all the purposes for which they are suited, and so make ourselves masters and possessors of nature. This would not only be desirable in bringing about the invention of an infinity of devices to enable us to enjoy the fruits of agriculture and all the wealth of the earth without labor, but even more so in (575) conserving health, the principal good and the basis of all other goods in this life. For the mind is so dependent upon the humors and the condition of the organs of the body that if it is possible to find some way to make men [in general] wiser and more clever than they have been so far, I believe that it is in medicine that it should be sought. It is true that medicine at present contains little of such great value; but without intending to belittle it, I am sure that everyone, even among those who follow the profession, will admit that everything we know is almost nothing compared with what remains to be discovered, and that we might rid ourselves of an infinity of maladies of body as well of mind, and perhaps also of the enfeeblement of old age, if we had sufficient understanding of the causes ⟨from which these ills arise⟩ and of all the remedies which nature has provided. It was my intention to [63] devote my whole life to the pursuit of this much-needed service, and I had found a method which, it seemed to me, should infallibly lead me to it unless I was prevented either by the brevity of life or the paucity of experiments. I judged that the best precaution against these two dangers would be to publish faithfully to the world the little which I had discovered, and to urge men of ability to continue the work by contributing, each one according to his inclinations and abilities, to the experiments which must be made. I hoped that each one would publish whatever he had learned, so that later investigators could begin where the earlier had left off. In this way mankind would combine the lives and work of many people, and would go much further than any individual could go by himself.

I noticed that experimentation becomes more necessary in proportion as we advance in knowledge. In beginning an investigation it is better to restrict ourselves to our usual experiences, which we cannot ignore if we pay any attention to them at all, than to seek rarer and more abstruse experiences. The reason for this is that these latter are often deceiving when the causes of the more common phenomena are still unknown, as the circumstances on which they depend are almost

always so particular and so minute that it is very difficult to
discover them. My own procedure has been the following: I
first tried to discover the general [64] principles or first causes
of all that exists or could exist in the world, without taking
any causes into consideration but God as creator, and without
using any evidence save certain indications of the truth which
we find in our own minds. After that I examined what were
the first and commonest effects which could be deduced from
these causes; and it seems (576) to me that by this procedure I
discovered skies, stars, an earth, and even, on the earth, water,
air, fire, minerals, and several other things which are the commonest of all and the most simple, and in consequence the
easiest to understand. Then, when I wanted to descend to
particulars, it seemed to me that there were so many different
kinds that I believed it impossible for the human mind to
distinguish the forms or species of objects found on earth from
an infinity of others which might have been there if God
had so willed. It thus appeared impossible to proceed further
deductively, and if we were to understand and make use of
things, we would have to discover causes by their effects, and
make use of many experiments. In consequence, reviewing in
my mind all the objects which had ever been presented to my
senses, I believe I can say that I have never noticed anything
which I could not explain easily enough by the principles I
had found. But I must also admit that the powers of nature
are so ample and vast, and that these principles are so simple
and so general, that I hardly ever observed a particular effect
without immediately recognizing [65] several ways in which it
could be deduced. My greatest difficulty usually is to find
which of these is the true explanation, and to do this I know
no other way than to seek several experiments such that their
outcomes would be different according to the choice of hypotheses.

For the rest, I have now reached the point, it seems to me,
where I see clearly enough the direction in which we should
go in this research; but I also see that the character and the
number of experiments required is such that neither my time

nor my resources, were they a thousand times greater than they are, would suffice to do them all. In proportion, therefore, to the opportunity I shall have in the future to do more or fewer of them, I will advance more or less in the understanding of nature. This I expected to convey in my treatise, and I hoped to show so clearly how useful my project might be that I would oblige all those who desire human benefit, all those who are truly virtuous and not merely so in ⌐affectation or⌐ reputation, both to communicate to me the experiments that they have already made and to assist me in the prosecution of what remained to be done.

But since then other reasons occurred to me which have made me change my mind. I still think that I should continue to write everything that I consider important as soon as I discover its truth, and do so with as much care as if I intended to publish it. In this way [66] I will have additional opportunities to examine my ideas, for doubtless we always scrutinize more closely that which we expect to be read by others (577) than that which we do for ourselves alone, and frequently the ideas which seemed true to me when I first conceived them have appeared false when I wished to put them on paper. Also, I would thus lose no opportunity to benefit humanity, if I am capable of it; and if my writings have any value, those into whose hands they fall after my death may use them as may be most appropriate. But I decided that I should never consent to have them published during my life, for fear that the opposition and controversy which they might arouse, and the reputation which they might possibly bring me, would cause me to waste time which I plan to use in research. For although it is true that each man is obligated to do as much as he can for the benefit of others, and that to be of no use to anyone is really to be worthless, yet it is also true that our interest should extend beyond the present time, and that it is well to avoid things which may bring some profit to the living when it is done with the intention of profiting our descendants still more. So I want it to be understood that the little I have learned thus far is a mere nothing compared to

what I do not know and yet do not despair of learning. For it
is much the same with those who gradually discover truth in
the [67] sciences as with those who, beginning to be rich, find
it less difficult to make important acquisitions than they
formerly did, when poorer, to make much smaller ones. Or
perhaps we should make the comparison with army chieftains,
whose forces usually grow in proportion to their victories and
who need more skill to maintain themselves after a defeat than
they do to win cities and whole provinces after a victory. For
to try to conquer all the difficulties and errors which stand in
our way when we try to reach the truth is really to engage in
battle; and to reach a false conclusion on an important issue
is to lose the battle. After such a loss, much more ability is
needed to reinstate ourselves in our former position than is
required to make great progress when we have already acquired well-tested principles. For myself, if I have thus far
found some truths in the sciences, and I trust that the treatises
contained in this volume [1] will convince the reader that I
have, I can say that these are only the ⌈results and⌉ consequences of five or six principal difficulties which I have sur-
mounted. These I count as so many battles in which fortune
has been on my side. I would even go so far as to say that I
think that two or three further victories of equal importance
would enable me to reach my goal, and I am not so old that I
cannot look forward to enough leisure, in the ordinary course
of nature, for this purpose. [68] But I feel the greater obligation (578) to make good use of the time remaining to me, the
more hope I have of being able to do so effectively, and I
would no doubt find many occasions to waste time if I published the foundations of my physics. For although my principles are almost all so evident that to hear them is to believe
them, and although there are none that I do not believe I can
demonstrate, nevertheless, as they could not possibly agree
with all the various opinions held by men at large, I foresee
that I would often be distracted by the opposition which they
would arouse.

[1] Optics, Meteorology, and Geometry.

One might argue that this opposition would be useful, partly to show me my mistakes, partly so that if there were anything worth while in my ideas, others would learn of it; and as many can see more than one, they would assist me immediately by their insight. But while I recognize that I am extremely likely to make mistakes, and while I rarely have much confidence in the first thoughts that come to me, nevertheless my experience of the objections that may be raised against me does not lead me to expect much profit by them. For I have often been favored with the judgments both of those I took to be friends and of those whom I took to be indifferent, as well as of a few who were moved by malignity and envy to expose what affection would hide from 'the eyes of' my friends. Yet it has rarely happened that an objection was offered which I had not foreseen, except when it was [69] very far-fetched; so that I have hardly ever met a critic of my opinions who did not appear to me to be either less rigorous or less equitable than myself. Nor have I noticed that the arguments carried on in the schools have ever brought to light a truth which was previously unknown, for when each person tries to win, he is more concerned to make his views prevail by appearing to be right than he is to weigh the evidence for both sides. Those who have long been good trial lawyers do not therefore make better judges afterwards.

As for the advantages which others might derive from hearing my ideas, they could not be so very great, especially since my ideas are still in a stage where much more has to be done before they can be applied to practice. And I think I may say without vanity that if anyone can accomplish this, it should be myself rather than any other person. Not that there may not be many minds incomparably superior to my own, but that we never understand a thing so well, and make it our own, when we learn it from another as when we have discovered it for ourselves. This is so true in this instance that although I have often explained some of my opinions (579) to very intelligent people, who seemed to understand them very distinctly while I was speaking, nevertheless when they

retold them I have noticed that they have almost always so
changed them that I could no longer accept them as my own.
I should also like to take advantage of this occasion to [70]
request posterity never to believe that any ideas are mine unless I have divulged them myself. I am not at all surprised at
the extravagances attributed to the ancient philosophers whose
writings we do not possess, nor do I judge in consequence that
their ideas were unreasonable. They were the wisest men of
their time, so I presume that their ideas have been badly reported. We notice, also, that it has rarely happened that one
of their disciples has surpassed them, and I feel sure that the
most devoted of the contemporary followers of Aristotle would
consider themselves fortunate if they had as much knowledge
of nature as he had, even on the condition that they would
never have any more. They are like the ivy, which has no
tendency to climb higher than the trees which support it, and
often grows downward after it has reached the top. For it
seems to me that followers also decline; that is, they make
themselves somehow less wise than they would be if they ab-
stained from study when they are not satisfied to understand
what is intelligibly explained by their author, but insist on
finding in him the solutions of many problems of which he
says nothing, and of which he has perhaps never thought. Just
the same, their manner of philosophizing is very convenient
for those who have only very mediocre minds; for the obscurity of the distinctions and principles which they use
enables them to talk of all things as bravely as though they
understood them ⟨perfectly⟩, and to defend all they [71]
say against the deepest and cleverest thinkers, as there is no way
to convince them. In this they appear to me similar to a blind
man who wishes to fight on even terms with one who can see,
and so brings him to the back of some very dark cave. These
people, I may say, are interested in my abstaining from the
publication of my principles of philosophy; for since these are
very simple and evident, I would be doing much the same to
them as though I opened some windows and let the light of
day enter into that cave where they had retired to fight. But

even the best minds need not wish to know my principles; for
if they want to be able to talk about all things and gain the
reputation of being learned, they can accomplish this more
easily by being satisfied with the appearance of truth, which
can be found without much trouble in all sorts of matters,
than by seeking truth itself. Truth can be discovered only
little by little, and in a few subjects, so that he who pursues
truth is often obliged to admit his ignorance when discussing a
subject which he has not investigated. But if they prefer the
knowledge of a little truth to the vanity of seeming to know
everything, as is no doubt preferable, and (580) if they wish
to pursue a plan similar to mine, it is not necessary for me to
tell them anything more than I have already said in this
Discourse, for if they are capable of going further than I have
gone, they will be still more capable of finding for themselves
everything which I think I have found. This is especially true
because I have always proceeded in a natural order, so that it
is certain that what remains to be discovered is [72] more
difficult in itself and more recondite than what I have so far
encountered. They would also experience much less pleasure
in learning it from me than in discovering it for themselves.
In addition, they would thus acquire the habit of discovery
by seeking easy things first, and pass gradually and by degrees to more difficult ones—a habit which will prove much
more useful than all my information could possibly be. As
for myself, I am persuaded that if I had been taught in my
youth all the truths of which I have since sought demonstrations, and if I could have learned them without difficulty,
I might never have learned any others, or at least, I would
never have acquired the habit and ability that I believe I
possess, always to find new truths in proportion to the efforts
I make to find them. In a word, if there is one task in the
world that cannot be finished as well by another as by the
one who started it, it is this one ⟨in which I am occupied and⟩
at which I am working.

It is true that as far as the related experiments are concerned, one man is not enough to do them all; but he could

not usefully employ other hands than his own, unless those of
workers or other persons whom he could pay. Such people
would do, in the hope of gain, which is a very effective motive,
precisely what they were told. As for those volunteers who
might offer to do it out of curiosity or the desire to learn, besides the fact that ordinarily they are stronger in promises
than in performance and that they make nothing but beautiful proposals of which none ever succeeds, they [73] would
infallibly expect to be paid by the explanation of some difficulties, or at least in compliments and useless conversation,
which would necessarily consume ⌜so⌝ much of the time needed
for investigation ⌜that the assistance would be at a net loss⌝.
As for the experiments which others have already made, even
if they were willing to communicate them, which those who
call them secrets never do, they are for the most part so com-
plicated with unneeded details and superfluous ingredients
that it would be very difficult for the investigator to discover
their core of truth. Besides this, he would find almost all these
experiments so poorly explained or even false, because those
who performed them forced themselves to make them appear
conformable to their principles, that if some of them were useful, they could not counterbalance the time that would be
lost in picking them out. So even if there were someone in the
world who (581) could be recognized without question as capable of making the greatest and the most beneficial discoveries,
and even if in consequence all other men attempted by every
means to aid him in the accomplishment of his designs, I do
not see that they could do anything except contribute to the
costs of the necessary experiments, and see that his leisure is
not interrupted by the importunities of anyone. But I am not
so presumptuous as to promise anything extraordinary, nor do
I indulge in such vain fancies as to imagine that the public
ought to be much interested in my plans. Finally, I am not so
base in spirit that I would be willing to accept from anyone
[74] any favor which it might be thought I had not deserved.

All these considerations taken together made me decide,
three years ago, that I did not wish to publish the treatise

which I had on hand, and I even resolved never during my
lifetime to permit others to read any paper of such a general
nature that they might understand the foundations of my
physics. But two other reasons have occurred since which have
obliged me to submit herewith some detailed essays, and to
give the public some account of my doings and my plans. The
first reason is that if I did not do so, several people who knew
of my previous intention to publish several essays might suppose that my reasons for abstaining were less honorable than
they really are. For although I do not care too greatly for
reputation—I might even say that I dislike it insofar as I consider it destructive of peace of mind, which I esteem above all
things—nevertheless I have never tried to hide my actions as
though they were criminal. Neither have I made much effort
to remain unknown, partly because I would have thought I
was doing myself an injustice, partly because that would have
produced a certain disquiet unfavorable to that perfect peace
of mind which I desire. I have always tried to remain indifferent to having or not having a reputation, but since I could
not avoid having some kind, I thought I should at least do my
best to avoid a bad one. The other reason which has obliged
me to write [75] this is that I observe a constantly greater re-
tardation in my plan to enlighten myself, because of an infinity of experiments which I must do, so that it is impossible
for me to succeed without the aid of others. And although I
do not ⟨, like Suffenus,⟩ flatter myself enough to hope that the
public would be much interested in what I am doing, nevertheless I do not wish to be so remiss in upholding my own
interests as to give occasion to those who survive me to re-
proach me, some day, on the ground that I might have accomplished many much better things than I did if I had not
been too negligent to explain how others could contribute to
my designs. (582)

And I thought that it would be easy to choose some topics
which would not be too controversial, which would not force
me to divulge more of my principles than I wish to, and which
would demonstrate clearly enough what I could or could not

do in the sciences. It is not for me to say whether I have succeeded ⌐, and I do not wish to influence anyone's decisions by
speaking of my own writings⌐; nevertheless I should like to
request the reader to examine them. In order to add to the
opportunities of judging, I also request all who find some objections to my ideas to take the trouble to send them to my
publisher. He will inform me, and I shall try to have my replies published at the same time as the objections. By this
means the reader, seeing both together, will more easily judge
of the truth. For I do not promise ever to make lengthy replies, but only to admit my mistakes ⌐very⌐ frankly if I recognize them; or, [76] if I cannot recognize them, to say simply
what I believe to be required for the defense of what I have
written. But I shall not go on to explain any new material,
for fear of engaging in an endless chain of tasks.

If some of the matters I deal with at the beginning of *Optics*
and *Meteorology* should at first sight appear offensive, because
I call them hypotheses and do not try to prove them, let the
reader have the patience to read all of it with attention, and I
hope that he will be satisfied with the result. For it seems to
me that the arguments follow one another in such a way that,
just as the last principles are demonstrated by the first ones
which are their causes, so these first ones are reciprocally
demonstrated by the last which are their effects. And one must
not suppose that I have here committed the fallacy which
logicians call circular reasoning; for as experience makes most
of the effects very certain, the causes from which I deduce
them serve not so much to prove as to explain them. On the
contrary, the truth of the hypotheses is proved by the actuality
of the effects. And I have called them hypotheses only to let
it be known that although I think I can deduce them from
the first truths which I have previously explained, I expressly
desired not to make the deduction. For there are certain people who imagine that they can learn in one day all that another has thought in twenty years, as soon as he has only spoken
two or three words, and who are only the more subject to err
and less capable of truth as they are more penetrating and

lively of spirit. I should like to prevent [77] these people from building some extravagant philosophy on what they believe to be my principles, for the fault might be attributed to me. As for my real opinions, I do not apologize for their novelty, especially since I am sure that anyone who attends to the argument will find them so simple and so conformable to common sense that they will seem less extraordinary and strange than any other opinions that can be held on the same subjects. I do not claim, either, that I am original in any of these ideas, but only that I have never accepted them (583) because they were maintained by others, nor because they were not so maintained, but only because reason persuaded me of their truth.

And if the invention described in *Optics* cannot immediately be built, I do not think it is therefore faulty. Since much skill and practice are necessary in order to make and adjust the machines which I have described, without their having any defects, I would not be less astonished to find it successful on the first attempt than I would be if someone could learn to play the lute excellently in a single day, for the sole reason that he had been given some excellent sheet music. ⌈And if I write in French, which is the language of my country, rather than in Latin, which is that of my teachers, it is because I hope that those who rely purely on their natural intelligence will be better judges of my views than those who believe only what they find in the writings of antiquity. And those who combine good sense with studiousness, whom alone I wish for [78] my judges, will not, I am sure, be so partial to Latin that they will refuse to accept my reasons because I explain them in the vulgar tongue.⌉

For the rest, I do not wish to speak here in detail of the progress in the sciences which I hope to make in the future, nor to commit myself to any promise to the public which I am not sure of fulfilling. I shall therefore only say that I have resolved to employ as much of my life as remains wholly in trying to acquire some knowledge of nature, of such a sort that we may derive rules of medicine more certain than those which we have had up to the present. My inclinations are so far removed from any other plans, especially those which can be useful to some only by harming others, that if circumstances forced me to employ those plans, I do not think I would be capable of carrying them to a successful conclusion. The declaration I am here making will not, I well know, procure me any worldly advantages, but I have no desire for them; and I shall always consider myself more obligated to those by whose favor I shall enjoy uninterrupted leisure than I would be to those who offered me the most honorable office on earth.

THE MEDITATIONS CONCERNING FIRST
PHILOSOPHY

To ⌈those most learned and most illustrious
men,⌉ the Dean and Doctors of the Sacred
Faculty of Theology of Paris

Gentlemen:

My reason for offering you this work is so logical, and after
you have learned its plan you will also, I am sure, have so
logical a reason to take it under your protection, that I believe nothing will recommend it to you more than a brief
statement of what I herein propose to do.

I have always thought that the two questions, of God and
of the soul, were the principal questions among those that
should be demonstrated by ⌈rational⌉ philosophy rather than
theology. For although it may suffice us faithful ones to believe by faith that there is a God and that the human soul
does not perish with the body, (2) certainly it does not seem
possible ever to persuade those without faith to accept any religion, nor even perhaps any moral virtue, unless they can first
be shown these two things by means of natural reason. And
since in this life one frequently finds greater rewards offered
for vice than for virtue, few persons would prefer the just to
the useful if they were not restrained either by the fear of
God or by the expectation of another life. It is absolutely
true, both that we must believe that there is a God because it
is so taught in the Holy Scriptures, and, on the other hand,
that we must believe the Holy Scriptures because they come
from God. The reason for this is that faith is a gift of God,
and the very God that gives us the faith to believe other
things can also give us the faith to believe that he [5] exists.
Nevertheless, we could hardly offer this argument to those
without faith, for they might suppose that we were committing the fallacy that logicians call circular reasoning.

And truly I have noticed that you, ⌈gentlemen,⌉ along with
all other theologians, assure us not only that the existence of

God can be proved by natural reason, but also that we can infer from the Holy Scriptures that our knowledge of God is much ⌐clearer ⌐and⌐ easier⌐ than our knowledge of various created things, ⌐so clear⌐ in fact, ⌐so absolutely easy to attain,⌐ that those who do not possess it are blameworthy. This is evidenced in the words of the Book of the Wisdom of Solomon, Chapter XIII, where it is said: "Howbeit they are not to be excused; for if their understanding was so great that they could discern the world and the creatures, why did they not rather find out the Lord thereof?" And in the Epistle to the Romans, Chapter I, where it is said that they are "without excuse," and again in the same place in these words: "That which may be known of God is manifest in them." It seems that we are being told that all that can be known of God can be demonstrated by reasons that we do not need to seek elsewhere than in ourselves, and that our minds alone are capable of furnishing us. That is why I have believed that it would not be inappropriate if I showed here how that can be done, and by what means we can know God more easily and more certainly than we know the things of the world.

And as for the soul, many have believed that it is not easy to understand its nature, (3) and some have even dared to say that human reasoning would convince us that it perishes with the body, and that faith alone can teach us the contrary. Nevertheless, as the Lateran Council, held under Leo X, Session 8, condemns these persons, and expressly orders Christian philosophers to refute their arguments and to employ all their intellectual abilities to make the truth known, I have decided to make the attempt in this work.

Moreover, the principal reason why many outside the Church do not wish to believe that there is a God and that the human soul is distinct from the body is that they claim that no one has so far been able to demonstrate these two things. I do not share their opinion; on the contrary, I hold that almost all of the arguments brought to bear on these two questions by so many illustrious men [6] are valid demonstrations when they are properly understood, and that it is practically impossible to invent new ones. So I believe that there is nothing more useful to be done in philosophy than ⌈critically and⌉ carefully to seek out, once and for all, the best ⌈and most reliable⌉ of such arguments, and to give them so clear and exact a presentation that it would thenceforward be evident to everyone that they are valid demonstrations. And finally, several persons have urged me to do this, since they knew that I have been practicing a certain method of solving all sorts of difficulties in the sciences—a method which really is not new, for nothing is older than the truth, but which they knew I was using rather successfully in other matters. I have therefore considered it my duty to see what I could achieve in this field. (4)

I have put in this treatise everything that I was able to discover about this subject. That is not to say that I have collected here all the various arguments which might be adduced as proofs in our subject, for I have never thought that that would be necessary unless no certain proof existed. I have only treated here of the most basic and principal ones in such a way that I can reasonably venture to maintain that they are very evident and very certain demonstrations. And I shall say further that they are such that I do not think there is any way in which the human mind can ever find better ones; for the importance of the subject, and the glory of God, to which all this relates, constrain me to speak somewhat more freely of myself here than I usually do. Nevertheless, whatever certainty and obviousness I find in my own arguments, I cannot convince myself that everyone will be able to understand them. There is a similar situation in geometry, where there are several proofs, left to us by Archimedes, Apollonius, Pappus, and several others, that are accepted by everyone as very certain and evident because they contain nothing but what, considered separately, is very easy to understand, and because there is no place where the consequences do not have an exact connection with and dependence upon their antecedents. Nevertheless, because these proofs are rather long and demand undivided attention, they are comprehended and understood by only a very few persons. In the same way, although I consider that the arguments I use here equal or even surpass in certainty and obviousness the [7] demonstrations of geometry, I nevertheless appreciate that they cannot be sufficiently well understood by many persons, partly because they also are somewhat lengthy and involved, but principally because they require a mind entirely free of all prejudice and one that can readily free itself from its attachment to the senses. And to tell the truth, there are not so many people in the world who are fitted for metaphysical speculations as there are those who are fitted for geometry. (5) There is this further difference, that in geometry everyone is persuaded that nothing should be written for which there is no certain proof. Therefore, those who are not well versed in the field are much more apt to make the mistake of accepting false demonstrations in order to make others believe that they understand them than they are to make the mistake of rejecting good ones. It is different in philosophy, where it is believed that there is nothing about which it is not possible to argue on either side. Thus few people engage in the search for truth, and many, who wish to acquire a reputation as clever thinkers, bend all their efforts to arrogant opposition to the most obvious truths.

That is why, ⌐gentlemen,⌐ since my arguments belong to philosophy, however strong they may be, I do not suppose that they will have any great effect unless you take them under your protection. But the esteem which everyone has for your Faculty is so great, and the name of the Sorbonne carries such authority, that not only is it more deferred to in matter of faith than any other group except the sacred councils, but even in human philosophy everyone agrees that it is impossible to find anywhere else so much reliability and knowledge, as well as prudence and integrity in the pronouncement of a judgment. Therefore, I do not doubt that if you will deign to give enough attention to this work so as to correct it—for, knowing not only my human fallibility but also my ignorance, I would not dare to affirm that it was free of error—and then to add to it whatever it lacks, to complete whatever is imperfect, and yourselves either to take the trouble to give a more adequate explanation of those points that need it or at least to advise me of them so that I may work on them; and finally, after the reasons by which I prove that there is a God and that the human soul differs from the body have been brought [8] to such a degree of clarity and obviousness, which I am sure is possible, (6) that they should be considered very exact demonstrations, if you then will deign to give them the authority of your approbation and publicly testify to their truth and certitude—I do not doubt, I say, that when this has been done, all the errors and false opinions which have ever been entertained on these two questions will soon be effaced from the minds of men. For the expression of the truth will cause all learned and wise men to subscribe to your judgment, and your authority will cause the atheists, who are ordinarily more arrogant than learned and judicious, to set aside their spirit of contradiction, or perhaps themselves defend the arguments which they see being accepted as demonstrations by all intelligent people, for fear of appearing not to understand them. And finally, everyone else will easily accept the testimony of so many witnesses, and there will no longer be anyone who dares to doubt the existence of God and the real and true distinction between the human soul and the body.

It is for you, ⌐who now see the disorders which doubt of these things produces,⌐ ⌐in your great wisdom\ to judge the fruit which would grow out of such belief, once it were well established; but it would not be fitting for me further to commend the cause of God and religion to those who have always been the firmest supporters ⌐of them ⌐and⌐ of the Catholic Church\. (7) [9]

PREFACE

I have already touched upon these two questions of God and of the human soul in the *Discourse on the Method of Rightly Conducting the Reason and Seeking Truth in the Sciences,* which I published in French in the year 1637. Then I was not concerned to give a complete discussion of the subjects, but only to treat of them in passing, in order to learn from the judgments of the readers in what way I should treat them afterward. For these questions have always seemed to me so important that I judged it appropriate to deal with them more than once. And the road I take to explain them is so little traveled and so far from the ordinary route that I did not think it would be useful to explain it in French in a discourse that might be read by anyone, for fear that those of feeble intellect would think it permissible for them to make the same attempt.

In the *Discourse on Method,* I requested everyone who found in my writings something worthy of criticism to do me the favor of informing me thereof. There were no noteworthy objections concerning these subjects except two, to which I shall here make a short reply before undertaking a more detailed presentation of them later.

The first objection is that it does not follow from the fact that the human mind, reflecting upon its own nature, (8) knows itself solely as a thinking being, that its nature or essence is only to think. The trouble is that this word "only" excludes all those other qualities that might perhaps also pertain to the nature of the mind.

To this objection I reply that it was not my intention at this point to exclude those qualities from the realm of objective reality, with which I was not then concerned, but only

(8)   67

from the realm of my thought. My intention was to say that I knew nothing to pertain to my essence except that I was a being which thinks, that is, a being having in itself the faculty of thinking. Nevertheless, I shall show further on how it follows from the fact that I know nothing else which belongs to my essence that nothing else really does belong to it.

The second objection is that it does not follow from the fact that I have in my mind the idea of a thing more perfect than I am that this idea is more perfect than myself, much less that what is represented by this idea exists.

But I reply that in this word "idea" there is here an equivocation. For it can be taken materially, as an operation of my intellect, and in this sense it cannot be said to be more perfect than myself; or it can be taken objectively for the body which is represented by this operation, which, even though it is not supposed to exist outside of my understanding, can nevertheless be more perfect than myself in respect to its essence. In the rest of this treatise I shall show more fully how it follows from the mere fact that I have in my mind an idea of something more perfect than myself that this thing really exists.

In addition, I have seen two other rather long works on this subject which did not so much oppose my reasons as my conclusions, and this by arguments drawn from the commonplaces of the atheists. (9) But since arguments of this type cannot make any impression in the minds of those who fully understand my reasoning, and since the judgment of many persons is so weak and irrational that they much more often let themselves be convinced by the first opinions they hear on a subject, however false and unreasonable they may be, than by a refutation of their opinions which is valid and true but which is heard later, I do not wish to reply to the arguments here, for fear of being obliged first to report them.

I shall only say, in general, that the arguments which atheists use to combat the existence of God always depend either upon the assumption that God has human characteristics, or

else upon the assumption that our own minds have so much
ability and wisdom that we presume to delimit and comprehend what God can and should do. Thus all that atheists al-
lege will give us no difficulty if only we remind ourselves that
we should consider our minds to be finite and limited, and
God to be an infinite and incomprehensible Being.

Now, having paid sufficient attention to the opinions of
men, I undertake directly to treat of God and of the human
mind, and at the same time to lay the foundations of first philosophy. I do this without expecting any praise for it from the
vulgar, and without hoping that my book will be read by
many. On the contrary, I would not recommend it to any except to those who would want to meditate seriously along
with me, and who are capable of freeing the mind from attachment to the senses and clearing it entirely of all sorts of
prejudices; and I know only too well that there are very few
people of this sort. But as for those who do not care much
about the order and connection of my arguments, and who
amuse themselves by making clever remarks on the several
parts, as (10) some will do—those persons, I say, will not profit
much from reading this work. And although they may find
opportunities for caviling in many places, they will hardly be
able to make any objections which are important or which are
worthy of reply.

And since I do not promise others to satisfy them wholly at
the first attempt, and since I do not so far presume as to believe that I can foresee all that may entail difficulties for some
people, I shall first present in these *Meditations* the same
thoughts by which I think I have reached a certain and evident knowledge of the truth, in order to see whether I will be
able to persuade others by means of the same reasons that
have persuaded me. After that I shall reply to the objections
which have been offered to me by people of insight and learning to whom I sent my *Meditations* to be examined before
committing them to the press. These have been so numerous
and so varied that I feel secure in believing that it would be

difficult for anyone else to find an objection of consequence that has not already been treated.

That is why I beg my readers to suspend their judgment upon the *Meditations* until they have taken the trouble of reading all these objections and the replies that I have made to them. (11)

SYNOPSIS OF THE SIX FOLLOWING
MEDITATIONS

In the First Meditation, I offer the reasons why we can doubt all things in general, and particularly material objects, at least as long as we do not have other foundations for the sciences than those we have hitherto possessed. And although it is not immediately apparent that so general a doubt can be useful, it is in fact very much so, since it delivers us from all sorts of prejudices and makes available to us an easy method of accustoming our minds to become independent of the senses. Finally, it is useful in making it subsequently impossible to doubt those things which we discover to be true after we have taken doubt into consideration.

In the Second, the mind,[1] which in its intrinsic freedom supposes that everything which is open to the least doubt is nonexistent, recognizes that it is nevertheless absolutely impossible that it does not itself exist. This is also of the highest utility, since by this means the mind can easily distinguish between those qualities which belong to it—that is to say, to its intellectual nature—and those which belong to the body.

But because it might happen that some persons will expect me to offer at this point reasons to prove the immortality of the soul, I think it my duty to warn them now (13) that, since I have tried to write nothing in this treatise for which I did not have very exact demonstrations, I have found myself obliged to follow an order similar to that used by geometricians, which is to present first all those things on which the proposition one is seeking to prove depends, before reaching any conclusions about the proposition itself.

But the first and principal thing required in order to recognize the immortality of the soul[2] is to form the clearest possi-

---

1 [Latin: *mens;* French: *esprit.*]
2 [L. *anima;* F. *âme.*]

ble conception of it, [10] and one which is entirely distinct from all the conceptions one can have of the body, which has been done in this Second Meditation. It is necessary, in addition, to know that all things which we conceive clearly and distinctly are true in the manner in which we conceive them, and this cannot be proved before the Fourth Meditation. Furthermore, we must have a distinct conception of corporeal nature, which we acquire partly in the Second, and partly in the Fifth and Sixth Meditations. And finally, we must conclude from all this that things which we clearly and distinctly perceive to be diverse substances, as we conceive the mind and the body, are in fact substances which are really distinct from each other; which is what we conclude in the Sixth Meditation. This is confirmed again, in the same Meditation, by the fact that we cannot conceive any body except as divisible, while the mind or soul of man can only be conceived as indivisible. For in reality we cannot conceive of half of any soul, as we can of the smallest possible body, so that we recognize that their natures are not only different but even in some sense contrary. I have not treated this subject further in this treatise, partly because we have already discovered enough to show with sufficient clarity that the corruption of the body does not entail the death of the soul, and so to give men the hope of a second life after death; and partly because the premises from which the immortality of the soul may be concluded depend upon the explanation of the whole of physics. First, (14) we must know that all substances in general—that is to say, all those things which cannot exist without being created by God—are by nature incorruptible and can never cease to be, unless God himself, by denying them his usual support, reduces them to nothingness. And secondly, we must notice that body, taken in general, is a substance, and that it therefore will never perish. But the human body, however much it may differ from other bodies, is only a composite, produced by a certain configuration of members and by other similar accidents, whereas the human soul is not thus dependent upon any accidents, but is a pure substance. For even if all its accidents change—as, for example, if it conceives of certain things, wills others, and receives sense impressions of still others—nevertheless it still remains the same soul. But the human body becomes a different entity from the mere fact that the shape of some of its parts has been changed. From this it follows that the human body may very easily perish, but that the mind ⌈or soul of man, between which I find no distinction,⌉ is immortal by its very nature. [11]

In the Third Meditation, I have explained at sufficient length, it seems to me, the principal argument I use to prove the existence of God. Nevertheless, I did not want to use at that point any comparisons drawn from physical things, in order that the minds of the readers should be as far as possible withdrawn from the use of and commerce with the senses. There may, therefore, be many obscurities remaining, which I hope will be completely elucidated in my replies to the objections which have since been made to me. One of these obscurities is this: how can the idea of a supremely perfect Being, which we find in ourselves, contain so much objective reality, ⌈that is to say, how can it participate by representation in so many degrees of being and of perfection,⌉ that it must have come from a supremely perfect cause? This I have explained in these replies by means of a comparison with a very ⌈⌈ingenious and⌉⌉ artificial machine, the idea of which occurs in the mind of some worker. For as the real cleverness of this idea must have some cause, I conclude it to be either the knowledge of this worker or that of some other from whom he has received this idea. In the same way (15) it is impossible that the idea of God, which is in us, does not have God himself as its cause.

In the Fourth, it is proved that all things which we ⌈conceive ⌈⌈or⌉⌉ perceive⌉ very clearly and very distinctly are wholly true. At the same time I explain the nature of error or falsity, which nature we ought to discover, as much to confirm the preceding truths as to understand better those that follow. Nevertheless, it should be noticed that I do not in any way treat here of sin—that is, of error committed in the pursuit of good and evil—but only of that which occurs in the judgment and discernment of the true and the false; and that I do not intend to speak of beliefs which belong to faith or to the conduct of life, but only of those which pertain to speculative truth and which can be known by the aid of the light of nature alone.

In the Fifth Meditation, besides the explanation of corporeal nature in general, the existence of God is again demonstrated by a new argument. There may also be some difficulties in this argument, but the solution will be found in the replies to the objections which have been made to me. In addition, I show how it is true that even the certainty of geometrical demonstrations themselves depends on the knowledge of God.

Finally, in the Sixth, I distinguish the action of the understanding from that of the imagination, and the marks of this distinction are described. Here I show that the ⌐mind ⌐or⌐ soul⌐ of man is really distinct from the body, and that nevertheless it is so tightly bound and united with it that it [12] forms with it what is almost a single entity. All the errors which arise from the senses are here exposed, together with. the methods of avoiding them. And finally, I here bring out all the arguments from which we may conclude the existence of material things; not because I judge them very useful, in that they prove what (16) they do prove—namely, that there is a world, that men have bodies, and other similar things which have never been doubted by any man of good sense—but because, in considering these arguments more closely, we come to recognize that they are not as firm and as evident as those which lead us to the knowledge of God and of our soul, so that the latter are the most certain and most evident truths which can become known to the human mind. That is all that I had planned to prove in these *Meditations,* which leads me to omit here many other questions with which I have dealt incidentally in this treatise. (17) [13]

FIRST MEDITATION

CONCERNING THINGS THAT CAN BE DOUBTED

There is no novelty to me in the reflection that, from my earliest years, I have accepted many false opinions as true, and that what I have concluded from such badly assured premises could not but be highly doubtful and uncertain. From the time that I first recognized this fact, I have realized that if I wished to have any firm and constant knowledge in the sciences, I would have to undertake, once and for all, to set aside all the opinions which I had previously accepted among my beliefs and start again from the very beginning. But this enterprise appeared to me to be of very great magnitude, and so I waited until I had attained an age so mature that I could not hope for a later time when I would be more fitted to execute the project. Now, however, I have delayed so long that henceforward I should be ⌈afraid that I was⌉ committing a fault if, in continuing to deliberate, I expended time which should be devoted to action.

The present is opportune for my design; I have freed my mind of all kinds of cares; (18) ⌈I feel myself, fortunately, disturbed by no passions;⌉ and I have found a serene retreat in peaceful solitude. I will therefore make a serious and unimpeded effort to destroy generally all my former opinions. In order to do this, however, it will not be necessary to show that they are all false, a task [14] which I might never be able to complete; because, since reason already convinces me that I should abstain from the belief in things which are not entirely certain and indubitable no less carefully than from the belief in those which appear to me to be manifestly false, it will be enough to make me reject them all if I can find in each some ground for doubt. And for that it will not be necessary for me to examine each one in particular, which would

be an infinite labor; but since the destruction of the foundation necessarily involves the collapse of all the rest of the edi-
fice, I shall first attack the principles upon which all my
former opinions were founded.

Everything which I have thus far accepted as entirely true
⌈and assured⌉ has been acquired from the senses or by means
of the senses. But I have learned by experience that these
senses sometimes mislead me, and it is prudent never to trust
wholly those things which have once deceived us.

But it is possible that, even though the senses occasionally
deceive us about things which are barely perceptible and very
far away, there are many other things which we cannot reasonably doubt, even though we know them through the senses
—as, for example, that I am here, seated by the fire, wearing a
⌐winter⌐ dressing gown, holding this paper in my hands, and
other things of this nature. And how could I deny that these
hands and ⌐his body are mine, unless I am to compare myself
with certain lunatics (19) whose brain is so troubled and be-
fogged by the black vapors of the bile that they continually
affirm that they are kings while they are paupers, that they are
clothed in ⌐gold and⌐ purple while they are naked; or imagine
⌐that their head is made of clay, or⌐ that they are gourds, or
that their body is glass? ⌐But this is ridiculous;⌐ such men are
fools, and I would be no less insane than they if I followed
their example.

Nevertheless, I must remember that I am a man, and that
consequently I am accustomed to sleep and in my dreams to
imagine the same things that lunatics imagine when awake, or
sometimes things which are even less plausible. How many
times has it occurred that ⌐the quiet of⌐ the night made me
dream ⌐of my usual habits:⌐ that I was here, clothed ⌐in a
dressing gown⌐, and sitting by the fire, although I was in fact
lying undressed in bed! It seems apparent to me now, that I
am not looking at this paper with my eyes closed, that this
head that I shake is not drugged with sleep, that it is with design and deliberate intent that I stretch out this hand and
perceive it. What happens in sleep seems not at all as clear

and as distinct as all this. [15] But I am speaking as though I never recall having been misled, while asleep, by similar illusions! When I consider these matters carefully, I realize so clearly that there are no conclusive indications by which waking life can be distinguished from sleep that I am quite astonished, and my bewilderment is such that it is almost able to convince me that I am sleeping.

So let us suppose now that we are asleep and that all these details, such as opening the eyes, shaking the head, extending the hands, and similar things, are merely illusions; and let us think that perhaps our hands and our whole body are not such as we see them. Nevertheless, we must at least admit that these things which appear to us in sleep are like ʹpaintedˋ scenes ⌐and portraits⌐ which can only be formed in imitation of something ⌐real and⌐ true, and so, at the very least, these types of things—namely, eyes, head, hands, and the whole body—are not imaginary entities, but real and existent. For in truth painters, even when (20) they use the greatest ingenuity in attempting to portray sirens and satyrs in ⌐bizarre and⌐ extraordinary ways, nevertheless cannot give them wholly new shapes and natures, but only invent some particular mixture composed of parts of various animals; or even if perhaps ⌐their imagination is sufficiently extravagant that⌐ they invent something so new that nothing like it has ever been seen, and so their work represents something purely imaginary and ⌐absolutely⌐ false, certainly at the very least the colors of which they are composed must be real.

And for the same reason, even if these types of things—namely, ⌐a body,⌐ eyes, head, hands, and other similar things—could be imaginary, nevertheless, we are bound to confess that there are some other still more simple and universal concepts which are true ⌐and existent⌐, from the mixture of which, neither more nor less than in the case of the mixture of real colors, all these images of things are formed in our minds, whether they are true ⌐and real⌐ or imaginary ⌐and fantastic⌐.

Of this class of entities is corporeal nature in general and its extension, including the shape of extended things, their quantity, or size and number, and also the place where they are, the time that measures their duration, and so forth. [16] That is why we will perhaps not be reasoning badly if we conclude that physics, astronomy, medicine, and all the other sciences which follow from the consideration of composite entities are very dubious ⌈and uncertain⌉; whereas arithmetic, geometry, and the other sciences of this nature, which treat only of very simple and general things without concerning themselves as to whether they occur in nature or not, contain some element of certainty and sureness. For whether I am awake or whether I am asleep, two and three together will always make the number five, and the square will never have more than four sides; and it does not seem possible that truths ⌈so clear and⌉ so apparent can ever be suspected of any falsity ⌈or uncertainty⌉. (21)

Nevertheless, I have long held the belief that there is a God who can do anything, by whom I have been created and made what I am. But how can I be sure but that he has brought it to pass that there is no earth, no sky, no extended bodies, no shape, no size, no place, and that nevertheless I have the impressions of all these things ⌈and cannot imagine that things might be other than⌉ as I now see them? And furthermore, just as I sometimes judge that others are mistaken about those things which they think they know best, how can I be sure but that ⌈God has brought it about that⌉ I am always mistaken when I add two and three or count the sides of a square, or when I judge of something else even easier, if I can imagine anything easier than that? But perhaps God did not wish me to be deceived in that fashion, since he is said to be supremely good. But if it was repugnant to his goodness to have made me so that I was always mistaken, it would seem also to be inconsistent for him to permit me to be sometimes mistaken, and nevertheless I cannot doubt that he does permit it.

At this point there will perhaps be some persons who would prefer to deny the existence of so powerful a God, rather than to believe that everything else is uncertain. Let us not oppose them for the moment, and let us concede ⌈according to their point of view⌉ that everything which I have stated here about God is fictitious. Then in whatever way they suppose that I have reached the state of being that I now have, whether they attribute it to some destiny or fate or refer it to chance, or whether they wish to explain it as the result of a continual interplay of events ⌐or in any other manner⌐; nevertheless, since to err and be mistaken [17] is a kind of imperfection, to whatever degree less powerful they consider the author to whom they attribute my origin, in that degree it will be more probable that I am so imperfect that I am always mistaken. To this reasoning, certainly, I have nothing to reply; and I am at last constrained to admit that there is nothing in what I formerly believed to be true which I cannot somehow doubt, and this not for lack of thought and attention, but for weighty and well-considered reasons. Thus I find that, in the future, I should ⌈withhold and suspend my judgment about these matters, and⌉ guard myself no less carefully from be-lieving them than I should from believing what is manifestly false (22) if I wish to find any certain and assured knowledge ⌈in the sciences⌉.

It is not enough to have made these observations; it is also necessary that I should take care to bear them in mind. For these customary and long-standing beliefs will frequently re-cur in my thoughts, my long and familiar acquaintance with them giving them the right to occupy my mind against my will ⌈and almost to make themselves masters of my beliefs⌉. I will never free myself of the habit of deferring to them and having faith in them as long as I consider that they are what they really are—that is, somewhat doubtful, as I have just shown, even if highly probable—so that there is much more reason to believe than to deny them. That is why I think that I would not do badly if I deliberately took the opposite posi-tion and deceived myself in pretending for some time that all these opinions are entirely false and imaginary, until at last I will have so balanced my former and my new prejudices that they cannot incline my mind more to one side than the other, and my judgment will not be ⌜mastered and⌝ turned by bad habits from the ⌜correct perception of things ⌜and the⌝ straight road leading to the knowledge of the truth⌝. For I feel sure that I cannot overdo this distrust, since it is not now a question of acting, but only of ⌜meditating and⌝ learning.

I will therefore suppose that, not ⌜a true⌝ God, ⌜who is very good and⌝ who is the supreme source of truth, but a certain evil spirit, not less clever and deceitful than powerful, has bent all his efforts to deceiving me. I will suppose that the sky, the air, the earth, colors, shapes, sounds, and all other objective things ⌜that we see⌝ are nothing but illusions and dreams that he [18] has used to trick my credulity. I will consider (23) myself as having no hands, no eyes, no flesh, no blood, nor any senses, yet falsely believing that I have all these things. I will remain resolutely attached to this hypothesis; and if I cannot attain the knowledge of any truth by this method, at any rate ⌜it is in my power to suspend my judgment. That is why⌝ I shall take great care not to accept any falsity among my beliefs and shall prepare my mind so well for all the ruses of this great deceiver that, however powerful and artful he may be, he will never be able to mislead me in anything.

But this undertaking is arduous, and a certain laziness leads me insensibly into the normal paths of ordinary life. I am like a slave who, enjoying an imaginary liberty during sleep, begins to suspect that his liberty is only a dream; he fears to wake up and conspires with his pleasant illusions to retain them longer. So insensibly to myself I fall into my former opinions; and I am slow to wake up from this slumber for fear that the labors of waking life which will have to follow the tranquillity of this sleep, instead of leading me into the daylight of the knowledge of the truth, will be insufficient to dispel the darkness of all the difficulties which have just been raised.

SECOND MEDITATION

OF THE NATURE OF THE HUMAN MIND, AND THAT IT IS MORE EASILY KNOWN THAN THE BODY

Yesterday's Meditation has filled my mind with so many doubts that it is no longer in my power to forget them. Nor do I yet see how I will be able to resolve them; I feel as though (24) I were suddenly thrown into deep water, being so disconcerted that I can neither plant my feet on the bottom nor swim on the surface. I shall nevertheless make every effort to conform precisely to the plan commenced yesterday and put aside every belief in which I could imagine the least doubt, just as though I knew that it was absolutely [19] false. And I shall continue in this manner until I have found something certain, or at least, if I can do nothing else, until I have learned with certainty that there is nothing certain in this world. Archimedes, to move the earth from its orbit and place it in a new position, demanded nothing more than a fixed and immovable fulcrum; in a similar manner I shall have the right to entertain high hopes if I am fortunate enough to find a single truth which is certain and indubitable.

I suppose, accordingly, that everything that I see is false; I convince myself that nothing has ever existed of all that my deceitful memory recalls to me. I think that I have no senses; and I believe that body, shape, extension, motion, and location are merely inventions of my mind. What then could still be thought true? Perhaps nothing else, unless it is that there is nothing certain in the world.

But how do I know that there is not some entity, of a different nature from what I have just judged uncertain, of which there cannot be the least doubt? Is there not some God or some other power who gives me these thoughts? But I need not think this to be true, for possibly I am able to produce them myself. Then, at the very least, am I not an entity my-self? But I have already denied that I had any senses or any body. However, at this point I hesitate, for what (25) follows from that? Am I so dependent upon the body and the senses that I could not exist without them? I have just convinced myself that nothing whatsoever existed in the world, that there was no sky, no earth, no minds, and no bodies; have I not thereby convinced myself that I did not exist? Not at all; without doubt I existed if I was convinced ⌈or even if I thought anything⌉. Even though there may be a deceiver of some sort, very powerful and very tricky, who bends all his efforts to keep me perpetually deceived, there can be no slight-est doubt that I exist, since he deceives me; and let him de-ceive me as much as he will, he can never make me be noth-ing as long as I think that I am something. Thus, after having thought well on this matter, and after examining all things with care, I must finally conclude and maintain that this proposition: *I am, I exist,* is necessarily true every time that I pronounce it or conceive it in my mind.

But I do not yet know sufficiently clearly what I am, I who am sure that I exist. So I must henceforth take very great care that I do not incautiously mistake [20] some other thing for myself, and so make an error even in that knowledge which I maintain to be more certain and more evident than all other knowledge ⌈that I previously had⌉. That is why I shall now consider once more what I thought myself to be before I be-gan these last deliberations. Of my former opinions I shall re-ject all that are rendered even slightly doubtful by the argu-ments that I have just now offered, so that there will remain just that part alone which is entirely certain and indubitable.

What then have I previously believed myself to be? Clearly, I believed that I was a man. But what is a man? Shall I say a rational animal? Certainly not, for I would have to determine what an "animal" is and what is meant by "rational"; and so, from a single question, I would find myself gradually en-meshed in an infinity of others more difficult ⌈and more incon-venient⌉, and I would not care to waste the little time and

leisure remaining to me in disentangling such difficulties. I
shall rather pause here to consider the ideas which previously
arose naturally and of themselves (26) in my mind whenever I
considered what I was. I thought of myself first as having a
face, hands, arms, and all this mechanism composed of ⌐bone
and flesh ⌐and⌐ members⌐, just as it appears in a corpse, and
which I designated by the name of "body." In addition, I
thought of the fact that I consumed nourishment, that I
walked, that I perceived and thought, and I ascribed all these
actions to the soul. But either I did not stop to consider what
this soul was or else, if I did, I imagined that it was something
very rarefied and subtle, such as a wind, a flame, or a very
much expanded air which ⌐penetrated into and⌐ was infused
thoughout my grosser components. As for what body was, I
did not realize that there could be any doubt about it, for I
thought that I recognized its nature very distinctly. If I had
wished to explain it according to the notions that I then entertained, I would have described it somewhat in this way: By
"body" I understand all that can be bounded by some figure;
that can be located in some place and occupy space in such a
way that every other body is excluded from it; that can be
perceived by touch or sight or hearing or taste or smell; that
can be moved in various ways, not by itself but by some other
object by which it is touched ⌐and from which it receives an
impulse⌐. For to possess the power to move itself, and also to
feel or to think, I did not believe at all that these are attributes of corporeal nature; on the contrary, rather, I was astonished [21] to see a few bodies possessing such abilities.

But I, what am I, on the basis of the present hypothesis that
there is a certain spirit who is extremely powerful and, if I
may dare to say so, malicious ⌐and tricky⌐, and who uses all his
abilities and efforts in order to deceive me? Can I be sure that
I possess the smallest fraction of all those characteristics which
I have just now said belonged to the nature of body? (27) I
pause to consider this attentively. I pass and repass in review
in my mind each one of all these things—it is not necessary to
pause to take the time to list them—and I do not find any one

of them which I can pronounce to be part of me. Is it characteristic of me to consume nourishment and to walk? But if it is true that I do not have a body, these also are nothing but figments of the imagination. To perceive?[1] But once more, I cannot perceive without the body, except in the sense that I have thought I perceived various things during sleep, which I recognized upon waking not to have been really perceived. To think?[2] Here I find the answer. Thought is an attribute that belongs to me; it alone is inseparable from my nature.

I am, I exist—that is certain; but for how long do I exist? For as long as I think; for it might perhaps happen, if I totally ceased thinking, that I would at the same time completely cease to be. I am now admitting nothing except what is necessarily true. I am therefore, to speak precisely, only a thinking being, that is to say, a mind, an understanding,[3] or a reasoning being, which are terms whose meaning was previously unknown to me.

I am something real and really existing, but what thing am I? I have already given the answer: a thing which thinks. And what more? I will stimulate my imagination ⌈to see if I am not something else beyond this⌉. I am not this assemblage of members which is called a human body; I am not a rarefied and penetrating air spread throughout all these members; I am not a wind, ⌈a flame,⌉ a breath, a vapor, or anything at all that I can imagine and picture to myself—since I have supposed that all that was nothing, and since, without abandoning this supposition, I find that I do not cease to be certain that I am something.

But perhaps it is true that those same things which I suppose not to exist because I do not know them are really no different from the self which I do know. As to that I cannot decide; I am not discussing that question at the moment, since I can pass judgment only upon those things which are known to me: I know that I exist and I am seeking to discover what

[1] [L. *sentire;* F. *sentir.*]
[2] [L. *cogitare;* F. *penser.*]
[3] [L. *intellectus;* F. *entendement.*]

I am, that "I" that I know to be. Now it is very [22] certain
that this notion ⌈and knowledge of my being⌉, thus precisely
understood, does not depend on things whose existence (28) is
not yet known to me; and consequently ⌈and even more cer-
tainly⌉, it does not depend on any of those things that I
⌈⌈can⌉⌉ picture in my imagination. And even these terms, "picture" and "imagine," warn me of my error. For I would be
imagining falsely indeed were I to picture myself as something; since to imagine is nothing else than to contemplate
the shape or image of a bodily entity, and I already know
both that I certainly exist and that it is altogether possible
that all these images, and everything in general which is involved in the nature of body, are only dreams ⌈and illusions⌉.
From this I see clearly that there was no more sense in saying
that I would stimulate my imagination to learn more distinctly what I am than if I should say: I am now awake, and
I see something real and true; but because I do not yet perceive it sufficiently clearly, I will go to sleep on purpose, in
order that my dreams will show it to me with more truth and
evidence. And thus I know manifestly that nothing of all that
I can understand by means of the imagination is pertinent to
the knowledge which I have of myself, and that I must remember this and prevent my mind from thinking in this fashion, in order that it may clearly perceive its own nature.

But what then am I? A thinking being.[4] What is a thinking
being? It is a being which doubts, which understands, ⌈which
conceives,⌉ which affirms, which denies, which wills, which rejects, which imagines also, and which perceives. It is certainly
not a trivial matter if all these things belong to my nature.
But why should they not belong to it? Am I not that same
person who now doubts almost everything, who nevertheless
understands ⌈and conceives⌉ certain things, who ⌈is sure of
and⌉ affirms the truth of this one thing alone, who denies all
the others, who wills and desires to know more about them,
who rejects error, who imagines many things, sometimes even
against my will, and who also perceives many things, as

4 [L. *res cogitans;* F. *une chose qui pense.*]

through the medium of ⌐the senses ⌐or⌐ the organs of the body? Is there anything in all that which is not just as true as it is certain that I am and that I exist, even though I were always asleep (29) and though the one who created me directed all his efforts to deluding me? And is there any one of these attributes which can be distinguished from my thinking or which can be said to be separable from my nature? For it is so obvious that it is I who doubt, understand, and desire, that nothing could be added to make it more evident. And I am also certainly the same one who imagines; [23] for once more, even though it could happen that the things I imagine are not true, nevertheless this power of imagining cannot fail to be real, and it is part of my thinking. Finally I am the same being which perceives—that is, which observes certain objects as though by means of the sense organs, because I do really see light, hear noises, feel heat. Will it be said that these appearances are false and that I am sleeping? ⌐Let it be so; yet at the very least⌐ it is certain that it seems to me that I see light, hear noises, and feel heat. This much cannot be false, and it is this, properly considered, which in my nature is called perceiving, and that, again speaking precisely, is nothing else but thinking.

As a result of these considerations, I begin to recognize what I am ⌐somewhat better ⌐and⌐ with a little more clarity and distinctness⌐ than heretofore. But nevertheless ⌐it still seems to me, and⌐ I cannot keep myself from believing that corporeal things, images of which are formed by thought and which the senses themselves examine, are ⌐much⌐ more distinctly known than that indescribable part of myself which cannot be pictured by the imagination. Yet it would truly be very strange to say that I know and comprehend more distinctly things whose existence seems doubtful to me, that are unknown to me and do not belong to me, than those of whose truth I am persuaded, which are known to me, and which belong to my real nature ⌐—to say, in a word, that I know them better than myself⌐. But I see well what is the trouble: my mind ⌐is a vagabond who⌐ likes to wander and is not yet able to stay within the strict bounds of truth. Therefore, let us ⌜give it the rein once more ⸢and⸣ allow it every kind of liberty, (30) ⌜permitting it to consider the objects which appear to be external,⸣ so that when a little later we come to restrain it ⌜gently and⸣ at the right time ⸢and force it to the consideration of its own nature and of the things that it finds in itself⸣, it will more readily permit itself to be ruled and guided.

Let us now consider the ⌜commonest⌝ things, which are commonly believed to be the most distinctly known ⸢⌜and the easiest of all to know⸣⌝, namely, the bodies which we touch and see. I do not intend to speak of bodies in general, for general notions are usually somewhat more confused; let us rather consider one body in particular. Let us take, for example, this bit of wax which has just been taken from the hive. It has not yet completely lost the sweetness of the honey it contained; it still retains something of the odor of the flowers from which it was collected; its color, shape, and size are apparent; it is hard and cold; it can easily be touched; and, if you knock on it, it will give out some sound. Thus everything which can make a body distinctly known are found in this example.

But now while I am talking I bring it close to the fire. What remains of the taste evaporates; the odor vanishes; its color changes; its shape is lost; its size increases; it becomes liquid; it grows hot; one can hardly touch it; and although it is knocked upon, it [24] will give out no sound. Does the same wax remain after this change? We must admit that it does; no one denies it ⸢, no one judges otherwise⸣. What is it then in this bit of wax that we recognize with so much distinctness? Certainly it cannot be anything that I observed by means of the senses, since everything in the field of taste, smell, sight, touch, and hearing are changed, and since the same wax nevertheless remains.

The truth of the matter perhaps, as I now suspect, is that this wax was neither that sweetness of honey, nor that ⌜pleasant⌝ odor of flowers, nor that whiteness, nor that shape, nor that sound, but only a body which a little while ago appeared

to my senses under these forms and which now makes itself
felt under others. But what is it, to speak precisely, that I
imagine ⌐when I conceive it⌐ in this fashion? Let us consider
it attentively (31) and, rejecting everything that does not belong to the wax, see what remains. Certainly nothing is left
but something extended, flexible, and movable. But what is
meant by flexible and movable? Does it consist in my picturing that this wax, being round, is capable of becoming
square and of passing from the square into a triangular shape?
Certainly not; ⌐it is not that,⌐ since I conceive it capable of
undergoing an infinity of similar changes, and I could not
compass this infinity in my imagination. Consequently this
conception that I have of the wax is not achieved by the faculty of imagination.

Now what is this extension? Is it not also unknown? For it
becomes greater in the melting wax, still greater when it is
completely melted, and much greater again when the heat increases still more. And I would not conceive ⌐clearly and⌐
truthfully what wax was if I did not think that even this bit
of wax is capable of receiving more variations in extension
than I have ever imagined. We must therefore agree that I
cannot even conceive what this bit of wax is by means of the
imagination, and that there is nothing but my understanding [5] alone which does conceive it. I say this bit of wax in
particular, for as to wax in general, it is still more evident.
But what is this bit of wax which cannot be comprehended
except by ⌐the understanding, or by⌐ the mind? Certainly it is
the same as the one that I see, that I touch, that I imagine;
and finally it is the same as I always believed it to be from the
beginning. But what is here important to notice is that perception [6] ⌐,or the action by which we perceive,⌐ is not a vision,
a touch, nor an imagination, and has never been that, even
though it formerly appeared so; [25] but is solely an inspec-
tion by the mind, which can be imperfect and confused as it

[5] [L. *mens;* F. *entendement.*]
[6] [L. *perceptio;* F. *perception.*]

was formerly, or clear and distinct as it is at present, as I attend more or less to the things ⌜which are in it and⌝ of which it is composed.

Now I am truly astonished when I consider ⌜how weak my mind is and⌝ how apt I am to fall into error. For even though I consider all this in my mind without speaking, (32) still words impede me, and I am nearly deceived by the terms of ordinary language. For we say that we see the same wax if it is present, and not that we judge that it is the same from the fact that it has the same color or shape. Thus I might be tempted to conclude that one knows the wax by means of eyesight, and not uniquely by the perception of the mind. So I may by chance look out of a window and notice some men passing in the street, at the sight of whom I do not fail to say that I see men, just as I say that I see wax; and nevertheless what do I see from this window except hats and cloaks which might cover ⌜ghosts, or⌝ automata ⌜which move only by springs⌝? But I judge that they are men, and thus I comprehend, solely by the faculty of judgment which resides in my mind, that which I believed I saw with my eyes.

A person who attempts to improve his understanding beyond the ordinary ought to be ashamed to go out of his way to criticize the forms of speech used by ordinary men. I prefer to pass over this matter and to consider whether I understood what wax was more evidently and more perfectly when I first noticed it and when I thought I knew it by means of the external senses, or at the very least by common sense, as it is called, or the imaginative faculty; or whether I conceive it better at present, after having more carefully examined what it is and how it can be known. Certainly it would be ridiculous to doubt the superiority of the latter method of knowing. For what was there in that first perception which was distinct ⌜and evident⌝? What was there which might not occur similarly to the senses of the lowest of the animals? But when I distinguished the real wax from its superficial appearances, and when, just as though I had removed its garments, I consider it all naked, it is certain that although there might still be some error in my judgment, I could not conceive it in this fashion without a human mind. (33)

And now what shall I say of the mind, that is to say, of myself? For so far I do not admit in myself anything other than the mind. Can it be that I, who seem to perceive this bit of wax [26] so ⌈clearly and⌉ distinctly, do not know my own self, not only with much more truth and certainty, but also much more distinctly and evidently? For if I judge that the wax exists because I see it, certainly it follows much more evidently that I exist myself because I see it. For it might happen that what I see is not really wax; it might also happen that I do not even possess eyes to see anything; but it could not happen that, when I see, or what amounts to the same thing, when I think I see, I who think am not something. For a similar reason, if I judge that the wax exists because I touch it, the same conclusion follows once more, namely, that I am. And if I hold to this judgment because my imagination, or whatever other entity it might be, persuades me of it, I will still reach the same conclusion. And what I have said here about the wax can be applied to all other things which are external to me.

Furthermore, if the idea or knowledge of the wax seems clearer and more distinct to me after I have investigated it, not only by sight or touch, but also in many other ways, with how much more ⌈evidence,⌉ distinctness ⌈and clarity⌉ must it be admitted that I now know myself; since all the reasons which help me to know and conceive the nature of the wax, or of any other body whatsoever, serve much better to show the nature of my mind! And we also find so many other things in the mind itself which can contribute to the clarification of its nature, that those which depend on the body, such as the ones I have just mentioned, hardly deserve to be taken into account.

And at last here I am, having insensibly returned to where (34) I wished to be; for since it is at present manifest to me that even bodies are not properly known by the senses nor by the faculty of imagination, but by the understanding alone; and since they are not known in so far as they are seen or touched, but only in so far as they are understood by thinking, I see clearly that there is nothing easier for me to understand than my mind. But since it is almost impossible to rid oneself so soon of an opinion of long standing, it would be wise to stop a while at this point, in order that, by the length of my meditation, I may impress this new knowledge more deeply upon my memory. [27]

THIRD MEDITATION

OF GOD: THAT HE EXISTS

Now I shall close my eyes, I shall stop my ears, I shall disregard my senses, I shall even efface from my mind all the images of corporeal things; or at least, since that can hardly be done, I shall consider them vain and false. By thus dealing only with myself and considering what is included in me, I shall try to make myself, little by little, better known and more familiar to myself.

I am a thing which thinks, that is to say, which doubts, which affirms, which denies, which knows a few things, which is ignorant of many, ⌐which loves, which hates,⌐ which wills, which rejects, which imagines also, and which senses. For as I have previously remarked, although the things which I sense and which I imagine are perhaps nothing at all apart from me ⌐and in themselves⌐, I am nevertheless sure that those modes of thought which I call sensations and imaginations, (35) only just as far as they are modes of thought, reside and · are found with certainty in myself.

And in this short statement I think I have reported all that I truly know, or at least all that I have so far noticed that I know. Now, ⌐⌐in order to try to extend my knowledge further,'1 I shall 'be circumspect and' consider with care if I cannot still discover in myself some other bits of knowledge which I have not yet observed. I am sure that I am a thinking being; but do I not then know what is required to make me sure of something? Certainly, in this first conclusion, there is nothing else which assures me of its truth but the clear and distinct perception of what I affirm. But this would really not be sufficient to assure me that what I affirm is true if it could ever happen that something which I conceived just as clearly and distinctly should prove false. And therefore it seems to me that I can already establish as a general principle that everything which we conceive very clearly and very distinctly is wholly true.

I have, however, previously accepted and admitted several things as very certain and very obvious which I have nevertheless subsequently recognized to be doubtful and uncertain. What, then, were those things? They were the earth, the sky, the stars, and all the other things I perceived through the medium of my senses. But [28] what did I conceive [1] clearly ⌈and distinctly⌉ in them? Nothing, certainly, unless that the ideas or thoughts of those things were present to my mind. And even now I do not deny the occurrence of these ideas in me. But there was still another thing of which I was sure and which, because of my habit of believing it, I thought I perceived very clearly, although in truth I did not perceive it at all—namely, that there were things outside of myself from which these ideas came and to which they were completely similar. That was the point in which, perhaps, I was mistaken; or at any rate, even if my judgment was in accord with the truth, it was no knowledge of mine which produced the truth of my judgment.

But when I considered something very simple and very easy concerning arithmetic and geometry, (36) as, for example, that two and three joined together produce the number five, and other similar things, did I not conceive them at least sufficiently clearly to guarantee that they were true? Certainly, if

---

1 [L. *percipio;* F. *concevoir.*]

I have since judged that these things might be doubted, it was
for no other reason than that it occurred to me that some God
might perhaps have given me such a nature that I would be
mistaken even about those things that seemed most obvious to
me. Every time that this idea of the supreme power of a God,
as previously conceived, occurs to me, I am constrained to admit that it is easy for him, if he wishes it, to bring it about
that I am wrong even in those matters which I believe I perceive ⟨with the mind's eye⟩ with the greatest ⟨possible⟩ obviousness. And on the other hand, every time I turn to the
things I think I conceive very clearly, I am so convinced by
them that I am spontaneously led to proclaim: "Let him deceive me who can; he will never be able to bring it about that
I am nothing while I think I am something, or, it being true
that I now am, that it will some day be true that I have never
been, or that two and three joined together make more or less
than five, or similar things ⟨in which I recognize a manifest
contradiction ⌈and⌉ which I see clearly could not be otherwise
than as I conceive them⌉."

And certainly, since I have no reason to believe that there
is a God who is a deceiver, and since I have not yet even considered those reasons that prove that there is a God, the argument for doubting which depends only on this opinion is very
tenuous and, so to speak, metaphysical. But in order to remove it altogether I must examine whether there is a God as
soon as an opportunity occurs, and if I find that there is one I
must also investigate whether he can be [29] a deceiver; for as
long as this is unknown, I do not see that I can ever be certain of anything. And now, ⌈in order that I shall have an opportunity to examine this question without interrupting the
order of thought which I have proposed for myself, which is
to pass by degrees from the notions which I discover to be
most basic in my mind to those that I can discover afterward,⌉
⟨good order seems to demand that⟩ I should first classify all
(37) my thoughts into certain types and consider in which of
these types there is, properly, truth or error.

Among my thoughts some are like images of objects, and it

is to these alone that the name of "idea" properly applies, as when I picture to myself a man, or a chimera, or the sky, or an angel, or God ⌐himself⌐. Then there are others with different forms, as when I wish, or fear, or affirm, or deny. In these cases I do conceive something as the object of the action of my mind, but I also add something else by this action to the idea which I have of the entity; and of this type of thought, some are called volitions or emotions, and others judgments.

Now as far as ideas are concerned, if we consider them only in themselves and do not relate them to something else, they cannot, properly speaking, be false; for whether I imagine a sage or a satyr, it is no less true that I imagine the one than the other. Similarly, we must not fear to encounter falsity in the emotions or volitions; for even though I may desire bad things, or even things which never existed, nevertheless it is no less true on that account that I desire them. So there is nothing left but judgments alone, in which I must take very great care not to make a mistake. But the principal and most common error which can be encountered here consists in judging that the ideas which are in myself are similar to, or conformable to, things outside of myself; for certainly, if I considered the ideas only as certain modes ⌐or aspects⌐ of my thought, without intending them to refer to some other exterior object, they could hardly offer me a chance of making a mistake.

Among these ideas, some seem to be born with me, others to ⌐be alien to me and to⌐ come from without, (38) and the rest to be made ⌐and invented⌐ by myself. For I have the ability to conceive what is generally called a thing, or a truth, or a thought; and it seems to me that I do not conceive this from anything but my own nature. But if I now hear some noise, if I [30] see the sun, if I feel heat, I have hitherto judged that these feelings proceeded from some things which exist outside of myself; and finally, it seems to me that sirens, hippogriffs, and ⌐all other⌐ similar chimeras are fictions and inventions of my mind. Perhaps I might persuade myself that all these ideas are ⌐of the type of those I call⌐ alien ⌐and which come from without⌐, or perhaps they are all innate, or perhaps they might all be invented; for I have not yet clearly discovered their true origin. And what I must principally do at this point is to consider, concerning those which seem to me to come from objects outside of me, what evidence obliges me to believe that they resemble those objects.

The first of these reasons is that it seems to me that nature teaches me so, and the second that I have direct experience that these ideas are not dependent upon my will ⌐nor upon myself⌐. For often they come to me despite my wishes; just as now, whether I wish it or not, I feel heat, and for that reason I conclude that this sensation, or rather this idea, of heat is produced in me by something different from myself, namely, by the heat of the fire near which I am sitting. And I see nothing which appears more reasonable to me than to judge that this alien entity sends to me and imposes upon me its likeness rather than anything else.

Now I must see whether these reasons are sufficiently strong and convincing. When I say that it seems to me that nature teaches me so, I understand by this word "nature" only a certain inclination which leads me to believe it, and not the light of nature which makes me know that it is true. But these two expressions are very different from each other; for I could not doubt in any way what the light of nature made me see to be true, just as it made me see, a little while ago, that from the fact that I doubted I could conclude that I existed. And ⌐there is no way in which this could be doubted, because⌐ I have no other faculty or power to distinguish the true from the false which could teach me that what this light of nature shows me as true is not so, and in which I could trust as much as in the light of nature itself. (39) But as for inclinations, which also seem to me to be natural, I have often noticed, when it was a question of choosing between virtues and vices, that they led me to the bad no less than to the good; and for this reason I have not been inclined to follow them even in what concerns the true and the false. [31]

As for the other reason, which is that these ideas must come from elsewhere, since they do not depend upon my will, I do not find this convincing either. For just as the inclinations which we are now considering occur in me, despite the fact that they are not always in accord with my will, so perhaps there is in me some faculty or power adequate to produce these ideas without the aid of any external objects, even though it is not yet known to me; just as it has so far always seemed to me that when I sleep, these ideas are formed in me without the aid of the objects which they represent. And finally, even if I should agree that the ideas are caused by these objects, it does not necessarily follow that they should be similar to them. On the contrary, I have often observed in many instances that there was a great difference between the object and its idea. Thus, for example, I find in myself two completely different ideas of the sun: the one has its origin in the senses, and must be placed in the class of those that, as I said before, came from without, according to which it seems to me extremely small; the other is derived from astronomical considerations—that is, from certain innate ideas—or at least is formed by myself in whatever way it may be, according to which it seems to me many times greater than the whole earth. Certainly, these two ideas of the sun cannot both be similar to the same sun ⌐existing outside of me⌐, and reason makes me believe that the one which comes directly from its appearance is that which least resembles it.

All this makes me recognize sufficiently well that up to now it has not been by (40) a valid and considered judgment, but only by a blind ⌐and rash⌐ impulse, that I have believed that there were things outside of myself and different from my own being which, through the organs of my senses or by whatever other method it might be, sent into me their ideas or images ⌐and impressed upon me their resemblances⌐.

But there is still another path by which to seek if, among the things of which I possess ideas, there are some which exist outside of myself. If these ideas are considered only in so far as they are particular modes of thought, I do not recognize any ⌐difference or⌐ inequality among them, and all of them

appear to arise from myself in the same fashion. But considering them as images, of which some represent one thing and
some another, it is evident that they differ greatly among
themselves. For those that represent substances [32] are undoubtedly something more, and contain in themselves, so to
speak, more objective reality ⌈, or rather, participate by representation in a higher degree of being or perfection,⌉ than
those that represent only modes or accidents. Furthermore,
that by which I conceive a supreme God, eternal, infinite, ⌈im-
mutable,⌉ omniscient, omnipotent, and the universal creator of
all things that exist outside of himself—that idea, I say, certainly contains in itself more objective reality than do those
by which finite substances are represented.

Now it is obvious, according to the light of nature, that
there must be at least as much reality in the total efficient
cause as in its effect, for whence can the effect derive its
reality, if not from its cause? And how could this cause communicate reality to the effect, unless it possessed it in itself?

And from this it follows, not only that something cannot be
derived from nothing, but also that the more perfect—that is
to say, that which contains in itself more reality (41)—cannot
be a consequence of ⌈and dependent upon⌉ the less perfect.
This truth is not only clear and evident in regard to the effects which have ⌈what philosophers call⌉ actual or formal reality, but also in regard to the ideas where one considers only
⌈what they call⌉ objective reality. For example, the stone
which has not yet existed cannot now begin to be, unless it is
produced by a being that possesses in itself formally or eminently all that enters into the composition of stone ⌈—that is,
which contains in itself the same things as, or others more excellent than, those which are in stone⌉. Heat cannot be produced in a being that previously lacked it, unless by something which is of an order ⌈, a degree, or a type⌉ at least as
perfect as heat, and so forth. But still, in addition, the idea of
heat or of stone cannot be in me, unless it was put there by
something which contains in itself at least as much reality as I
conceive there is in heat or stone; for even though that cause

does not transfer to my idea anything of its actual or formal reality, we must not therefore suppose that such a cause is any less real, nor that the nature of an idea ⌐, since it is a work of the mind,⌐ is such that it does not require any other formal reality than what it receives and borrows from thought or mind, of which it is only a mode ⌐—that is, a way or manner of thinking⌐. In order that an idea should contain one particular objective reality rather [33] than another, it should no doubt obtain it from some cause in which there is at least as much formal reality as the idea contains objective reality. For if we suppose that there is some element in an idea which is not present in its cause, this element must then arise from nothing. However imperfect may be this mode of being, by which a thing exists objectively or is represented by a concept of it in the understanding, certainly we can nevertheless say that this mode and manner of being is not nothing, and consequently the idea cannot derive its origin from nothingness.

Nor must I imagine that, since the reality that I consider to be in my ideas is only objective, the same reality need not (42) be present formally ⌐or actually⌐ in the causes of these ideas, but that it is sufficient that it should be objectively present in them. For just as this manner of existing objectively belongs to ideas as part of their own nature, so also the manner or fashion of existing formally belongs to the causes of these ideas, or at the very least to their first and principal causes, as part of their own nature. And even though it might happen that one idea gives birth to another idea, that could not continue indefinitely; but we must finally reach a first idea, the cause of which is like an archetype ⌐or source⌐, in which is contained formally ⌐and in actuality⌐ all the reality ⌐or perfection⌐ that is found only objectively or by representation in the ideas. Thus the light of nature makes me clearly recognize that ideas in me are like paintings or pictures, which can, truly, easily fall short of the perfection of the original from which they have been drawn, but which can never contain anything greater or more perfect. And the longer and the more carefully I consider all these arguments, the more clearly and distinctly I know that they are true.

What, then, shall I conclude from all this evidence? Clearly, that if the objective reality ⌈᾿or perfection⌉ of some one of my ideas is such that I recognize clearly that this same reality ⌈᾿or perfection⌉ does not exist in me, either formally or eminently, and consequently that I cannot myself be its cause, it necessarily follows that I am not alone in the world, but that there is also some other entity that exists and is the cause of this idea. On the other hand, if I find no such idea in myself, I will have no argument which can convince me and make me certain of the existence of any entity other than myself; for I have diligently searched for all such arguments [34] and have been thus far unable to find any other.

Among all these ideas which exist in me, besides that which represents myself to myself, concerning which there can be no difficulty here, (43) there is another which represents a God, others corporeal and inanimate things, others angels, others animals, and still others which represent men similar to myself. But as far as the ideas which represent other men, or animals, or angels are concerned, I can easily imagine that they could be formed by the ⌈mixture and⌉ combination of my other ideas, ᾿of myself,᾿ of corporeal objects, and of God, even though outside of me there were no other men in the world, nor any animals, nor any angels. And as far as the ideas of corporeal objects are concerned, I recognize nothing in them so great ⌈or so excellent⌉ that it seems impossible that they could arise from myself. For if I consider them more closely and examine them in the same way that I examined the idea of wax yesterday, I find that there are only a few elements in them which I conceive clearly and distinctly—namely, size, or extension in length, width and depth; shape, which results from the termination and limitation of this extension; location, which the variously shaped objects have with respect to one another; and movement, or the changing of this location. To this one may add substance, duration, and number. As for other elements, such as light, colors, sounds, odors, tastes, heat, cold, and the other qualities involved in the sense of touch, they occur in my thought with so much obscurity and confusion that I do not even know whether they are true or false and only apparent, that is, whether my ideas of these qualities are really ideas of actual bodies or of non-bodies ⌐, which are only chimerical and cannot exist⌐. For even though I have previously stated that true and formal falsity can characterize judgments only, there can exist nevertheless a certain material falsity in ideas, as when they represent that which is nothing as though it were something. For example, my ideas of cold and heat are so little clear (44) and distinct that I cannot determine from them whether cold is only the absence of heat or heat the absence of cold, or whether both of them are real qualities, or whether neither is such. Besides, ⌐since ideas are like pictures,⌐ there can be no ideas which do not [35] seem to us to represent objects; and if it is true to say that cold is nothing but an absence of heat, the idea of cold which represents it as something real and positive could, not inappropriately, be called false, and so for other similar ideas.

And assuredly, it is not necessary for me to attribute to such ideas any other source than myself. For if they are false—that is, if they represent entities which do not exist—the light of nature lets me know that they proceed from nothingness; that is, that they occur in me only because something is lacking in my nature and that the latter is not altogether perfect. And if these ideas are true, nevertheless, since they show me so little reality that I cannot even ⌐clearly⌐ distinguish the object represented from the nonexistent, I do not see why they could not be produced by myself ⌐and why I could not be their author⌐.

As for my clear and distinct ideas of corporeal things, there are some of them which, it seems to me, might have been derived from my ideas of myself, such as my ideas of substance, duration, number, and other similar things. For I think that stone is a substance, or a thing which is capable of existing by itself, and that I myself am also a substance, even though I

understand perfectly that I am a being that thinks and
that is not extended, and that stone, on the contrary, is an
extended being which does not think. Nevertheless, even
though there is a notable difference between these two conceptions, they seem to agree in this fact that both of them
represent substances. In the same way, when I think I exist
now and remember in addition having existed formerly, or
when I conceive various thoughts of which I recognize the
number, I acquire (45) the ideas of duration and number
which I afterward am able to apply to any other things I
wish. As for the other qualities of which the ideas of material
entities are composed—namely, extension, shape, location, and
movement—it is true that they are not formally in my nature,
since I am only a thinking being; but since these are only particular modes of substance, ⌈or, as it were, the garments in
which corporeal substance appears to us,⌉ and since I am myself a substance, it seems that they might be contained in my
nature eminently.

Thus there remains only the idea of God, in which we must
consider if there is something which could not have come
from myself. By the word "God" I mean an infinite substance,
⌈eternal, immutable,⌉ [36] independent, omniscient, omnipotent, and that by which I myself and all other existent things,
if it is true that there are other existent things, have been
created and produced. But these attributes are ⌐such ⌈—they
are⌐ so great and so eminent—⌉ that the more attentively I
consider them, the less I can persuade myself that I could
have derived them from my own nature. And consequently we
must necessarily conclude from all that I have previously said
that God exists. For even though the idea of substance exists
in me from the very fact that I am a substance, I would nevertheless have no idea of an infinite substance, I who am a finite
being, unless the idea had been placed in me by some substance which was in fact infinite.

And I must not imagine that I do not conceive infinity as a
real idea, but only through the negation of what is finite in
the manner that I comprehend rest and darkness as the nega-

tion of movement and light. On the contrary, I see manifestly
that there is more reality in infinite substance than in finite
substance, and my notion of the infinite is somehow prior to
that of the finite, that is, the notion of God is prior to that of
myself. For how would it be possible for me to know that I
doubt and that I (46) desire—that is, that I lack something
and am not all perfect—if I did not have in myself any idea
of a being more perfect than my own, by comparison with
which I might recognize the defects of my own nature?

And we cannot say that this idea of God might be materially false, and that in consequence I might derive it from
nothingness, ⌐or, in other words, that it might be in me as a
deficiency,⌐ as I have just now said about the ideas of heat and
cold, and other similar things. For, on the contrary, this idea
is very clear and very distinct and contains more objective reality than does any other, so that there is no other which is
more true from its very nature, nor which is less open to the
suspicion of error and falsity.

This idea, I say, of a supremely perfect and infinite being,
is entirely true; for even though one might imagine that such
a being does not exist, nevertheless one cannot imagine that
the idea of it does not represent anything real, as I have just
said of the idea of cold. It is also very clear and very distinct,
since everything real and true which my mind conceives
clearly and distinctly, and which contains some perfection, is
contained and wholly included in this idea. [37] And this will
be no less true even though I do not comprehend the infinite
and though there is in God an infinity of things which I cannot comprehend, or even perhaps suggest in thought, for it is
the nature of infinity that I, who am finite and limited, cannot comprehend it. It is enough that I understand this and
that I judge that all qualities which I conceive clearly and in
which I know that there is some perfection, and possibly also
an infinity of other qualities of which I am ignorant, are in
God formally or eminently. Then the idea which I have of
God is seen to be the truest, the clearest, and the most distinct
of all the ideas which I have in my mind.

But possibly I am something more than I suppose myself to be. Perhaps all the perfections which I attribute to the nature of a God are somehow potentially in me, although they ⌐are not yet actualized and⌐ do not yet appear (47) and make themselves known by their actions. Experience shows, in fact, that my knowledge increases and improves little by little, and I see nothing to prevent its increasing thus, more and more, to infinity; nor ⌐even⌐ why, my knowledge having thus been augmented and perfected, I could not thereby acquire all the other perfections of divinity; nor finally, why my potentiality of acquiring these perfections, if it is true that I possess it, should not be sufficient to produce the ideas of them ⌐and introduce them into my mind⌐.

Nevertheless, ⌐considering the matter more closely, I see that⌐ this could not be the case. For, first, even if it were true that my knowledge was always achieving new degrees of perfection and that there were in my nature many potentialities which had not yet been actualized, nevertheless none of these qualities belong to or approach ⌐in any way⌐ my idea of divinity, in which nothing is merely potential ⌐and everything is actual and real⌐. Is it not even a most certain ⌐and infallible⌐ proof of the imperfection of my knowledge that it can ⌐grow little by little and⌐ increase by degrees? Furthermore, even if my knowledge increased more and more, I am still unable to conceive how it could ever become actually infinite, since it would never arrive at such a high point of perfection that it would no longer be capable of acquiring some still greater increase. But I conceive God to be actually infinite in such a high degree that nothing could be added to the ⌐supreme⌐ perfection that he already possesses. And finally, I understand ⌐very well⌐ that the objective existence of an idea can never be produced by a being that [38] is merely potential and that, properly speaking, is nothing, but only by a formal or actual being.

And certainly there is nothing in all that I have just said which is not easily known by the light of nature to all those who will consider it carefully. But when I relax my attention somewhat, my mind is obscured, as though blinded by the images of sensible objects, and does not easily recall the reason why my idea of a being more perfect than my own must necessarily have been imparted to me by a being that is actually more perfect. (48)

That is why I wish to pass on now to consider whether I myself, who have this idea of God, could exist if there had been no God. And I ask, from what source would I have derived my existence? Possibly from myself, or from my parents, or from some other causes less perfect than God; for we could ⌐think of or˥ imagine nothing more perfect, nor even equal to him. But if I were ⌐independent of anything else and were˥ the author of my own being, I would doubt nothing, I would experience no desires, and finally I would lack no perfection. For I would have endowed myself with all those perfections of which I had any notion, and thus I would be God ⌐himself˥.

And I must not imagine that what I lack might be more difficult to acquire than what I already possess; for, on the contrary, it is very certain that it was far more difficult for this ego—that is, this being or substance that thinks—to emerge from nothingness than it would be for me to acquire the ⌐insight into and˥ knowledge of various matters about which I am ignorant, since this knowledge would only be an accident of this substance. And certainly if I had given myself all the qualities that I have just mentioned and more, ⌐that is, if I were myself the author of my birth and of my being,˥ I would at least not have denied to myself those things which could be obtained with greater facility ⌐as are an infinity of items of information, of which my nature happens to be deprived˥. I would not even have denied myself any of the qualities which I see are included in the idea of God, because there is no one of them which seems to me to be more difficult to create or acquire. And if there were one of them which was more difficult, certainly it would have appeared so to me, because, on the assumption that all my other qualities were self-given, I would see in this one quality a limitation of my power ⌐since I would not be able to acquire it˥.

Even if I could suppose that possibly I have always been as I am now, still I could not evade the force [39] of this argument ⌐since it would not follow that no author of my existence need then be sought ⌐and˥ I would still have to recognize that it is necessary that God is the author of my existence˥. For the whole duration of my life can be divided into (49) an infinite number of parts, no one of which is in any way dependent upon the others; and so it does not follow from the fact that I have existed a short while before that I should exist now, unless at this very moment some cause produces and creates me, as it were, anew or, more properly, conserves me.

Actually it is quite clear and evident to all who will consider attentively the nature of time that a substance, to be conserved at every moment that it endures, needs the same power and the same action which would be necessary to produce it and create it anew if it did not yet exist. Thus the light of nature makes us see clearly that conservation and creation differ only in regard to our manner of thinking ⌐and not in reality˥.

It is therefore only necessary here for me to question myself and consider my own nature to see whether I possess some power and ability by means of which I can bring it about that I, who exist now, shall still exist a moment later. For since I am nothing but a being which thinks, or at least since we are so far concerned only with that part of me, if such a power resided in me, certainly I should at least be conscious of it ⌐and recognize it˥. But I am aware of no such thing, and from that fact I recognize evidently that I am dependent upon some ⌐other˥ being different from myself.

But possibly that being upon whom I am dependent is not God, and I am produced either by my parents or by some other causes less perfect than he. Not at all, that cannot be the case. For, as I have already said, it is very evident that there must be at least as much reality in the cause as in the effect; and since I am a being who thinks and who has some idea of God, whatever turns out to be the cause of my existence must be admitted to be also a being who thinks and which has in itself the idea of all the perfections which I attribute to ⌈the divine nature ⌐of⌐ God⌐. Thus we can in turn inquire whether this cause derives its ⌈origin and⌐ existence from itself or from something else. For if it is self-caused, it follows, for the reasons that I have previously given, that this cause must be God ⌐himself⌐, (50) since, to have the capacity to be or exist by itself, it must also, without doubt, have the power to possess in actuality all the perfections which it can imagine, that is, all those that I conceive [40] to be in God. But if it derives its existence from something else, we ask once more, for the same reason, whether this second cause is caused by itself or by another, until ⌈step by step⌐ we finally arrive at an ultimate cause which will ⌈turn out to⌐ be God. And it is very obvious that in this case there cannot be an infinite regress, since it is not so much a question of the cause which produced me in the past as of that which conserves me in the present.

Nor can we pretend that possibly several ⌐partial⌐ causes have concurred to produce me, and that from one of them I received the idea of one of the perfections which I attribute to God, and from another the idea of some other, so that each of these perfections would actually be found somewhere in the universe, but would nowhere be joined together ⌈and assembled⌐ in one entity which would be God. For, on the contrary, the unity, simplicity, or inseparability of all the qualities which are in God is one of the principal perfections which I conceive to be in him. And certainly the idea of this unity of all God's perfections could not have been placed in me by any cause from which I had not also received the ideas of all the other perfections. For nothing could have brought it about that I understood these qualities as joined together and inseparable, without having brought it about at the same time that I know what qualities they were ⌈and that I knew something about each one of them⌐.

Finally, concerning my parents, ⌈from whom it seems that I derive my birth,⌐ even if all that I could ever have believed of them should be true, that would still not imply that it is they

who conserve me, nor even that they made and produced me
in so far as I am a thinking being ⌐l, there being no relation
between the bodily activity by which I have been accustomed
to believe I was engendered and the production of a thinking
substance⌐l. The most that they can have contributed to my
birth is that they have produced certain arrangements in the
matter within which I have so far believed that the real I,
that is, my mind, (51) is enclosed. Thus the existence of my
parents is no objection to the argument, and we must necessarily conclude from the mere fact that I exist and that I have
an idea of a supremely perfect Being, or God, that the existence of God is very clearly demonstrated.

The only task left is to consider how I received this idea
⌐from God⌐; for I did not get it through the senses, nor has it
ever appeared to me unexpectedly, as the ideas of sensible objects are wont to do, when these objects are presented or seem
to be presented [41] to my external sense organs. Nor is it
only a product ⌐or fiction⌐ of my mind, for it is not in my
power to diminish it or to add anything to it. No possibility
remains, consequently, except that this idea is born and produced with me from the moment that I was created, just as
was the idea of myself.

And truly it must not be thought strange that God, in cre-
ating me, put this idea in my nature in much the same way
as an artisan imprints his mark on his work. Nor is it necessary that this mark be something different from the work itself. From the very fact that God has created me, it is very
credible that he has made me, in some sense, in his own image
and similitude, and that I conceive this similitude, in which
the idea of God is contained, by the same faculty by which I
conceive myself. In other words, when I reflect upon myself,
I not only know that I am ⌐an imperfect being,⌐ incomplete
and dependent upon some other being, and a being which
strives and aspires incessantly to become something better and
greater than I now am, but also and at the same time I know
that the being upon which I depend possesses in itself all
these great qualities ⌐to which I aspire and the ideas of which

I find in myself, and possesses these qualities⌉, not indefinitely and merely potentially, but ⌈really,⌉ actually, and infinitely, and so that it is God. And the whole force of the argument ⌈I have here used to prove the existence of God⌉ consists in the fact that I recognize that it would not be possible (52) for my nature to be what it is, possessing the idea of a God, unless God really existed—the same God, I say, the idea of whom I possess, the God who possesses all these ⌈high⌉ perfections of which my mind can have some ⌜slight⌝ idea, without however being able fully to comprehend them; who is subject to no defect ⌈and who has no part of all those qualities which involve imperfection⌉. And from this it is quite evident that he cannot be a deceiver, since the light of nature teaches us that deception must always be the result of some deficiency.

But before I examine this more carefully and pass on to the consideration of other truths which may follow from this one, it seems proper to pause for a while to contemplate this all-perfect God, to weigh at leisure his ⌈marvelous⌉ attributes, to consider, admire, and adore the ⌈incomparable⌉ beauty of this immense magnificence, as far at least as the power of my mind, which is somewhat overwhelmed by it, permits. [42]

For just as faith teaches that the supreme felicity of the next life consists only in this contemplation of divine majesty, so let us try from now on whether a similar contemplation, although incomparably less perfect, will not make us enjoy the greatest happiness that we are capable of experiencing in this life.

FOURTH MEDITATION

OF THE TRUE AND THE FALSE

In these last few days I have become so accustomed to ignoring my senses, and I have so carefully noticed that we know very little (53) with certainty about corporeal things and that we know much more about the human mind, and still more again about God himself, that it is easy for me now to turn my consideration from ⌈sensible or⌉ picturable things to those which, being wholly dissociated from matter, are purely intelligible. And certainly my idea of the human mind, in so far as it is a thinking being, not extended in length, breadth, and depth, and participating in none of the qualities of body, is incomparably more distinct than my idea of anything corporeal. And when I consider that I doubt, that is to say, that I am an incomplete and dependent being, the idea of a complete and independent being, that is, of God, occurs to my mind with very great distinctness and clearness. And from the very fact that such an idea occurs in·me, or that I who possess this idea exist, I so evidently conclude that God exists and that my own existence depends entirely upon him every moment of my life that I am confident that the human mind can know nothing with greater evidence and certainty. And I already seem to have discovered a path that will lead us from this contemplation of the true God, in whom all the treasures of science and wisdom are contained, to the knowledge of all other beings ⌈in the universe⌉.

For first, I recognize that it is impossible for God ever [43] to deceive me, since in all fraud and deception there is some kind of imperfection. And although it seems that to be able to deceive is a mark of ⧸acumen,⧹ ⌈subtlety,⌉ or power, nevertheless to wish to deceive testifies without question to weakness or malice, which could not be found in God.

Then, I know by my own experience that I have some ability to judge, ⌈⧸or to distinguish the true from the false,⧹⌉ an ability which I have no doubt received from God just as I have received all the other qualities ⧸which are part of me ⌈and⧹ which I possess⌉. (54) Furthermore, since it is impossible that God wishes to deceive me, it is also certain that he has not given me an ability of such a sort that I could ever go wrong when I use it properly.

And no doubt on this subject would remain, except that we could apparently then draw the conclusion that I can never commit an error. For if everything in me is derived from God, and if he has not given me any ability to make errors, it seems that I should never be mistaken. It is true that when I consider ⌐'myself'⌐ only ⌐'as a creature of'⌐ God, ⌐and when I orient myself completely upon him,⌐ I discover ⌐in myself⌐ no cause of error or falsity. But when, a little later, I think of myself, experience convinces me that I am nevertheless subject to innumerable errors. And when I try to discover the reason for this, I notice that there is present in my thought not only a real and positive idea of God, or rather of a supremely perfect being, but also, so to speak, a certain negative idea of nothingness, or of what is infinitely removed from every kind of perfection. And I see that I am, as it were, a mean between God and nothingness, that is, so placed between the supreme Being and not-being that, in so far as a supreme Being has produced me, there is truly nothing in me which could lead me into error; but if I consider myself as somehow participating in nothingness or not-being, that is, in so far as I am not myself the supreme being ⌐and am lacking many things⌐, ⌐I find myself exposed to an infinity of defects, so that⌐ I should not be astonished if I go wrong.

Thus I ⌐clearly⌐ recognize that error as such is not something real which depends upon God, but only a deficiency. Thus, in order to err, I do not need a faculty [1] which God has given to me expressly for the purpose; mistakes on my part occur because the power that God has given me to discriminate between the true and the false is not infinite.

Nevertheless I am not yet altogether satisfied, for error is not (55) a pure negation ⌐—that is, it is not a simple deficiency or lack of some perfection which is not my [44] due⌐, but rather a privation ⌐or lack⌐ of some knowledge which it seems to me that I should possess. And in considering the nature of God, it does not seem possible that he should have endowed me with any faculty [2] which is not perfect of its kind, or which

---

[1] [L. facultas; F. puissance.]
[2] [L. facultas; F. faculté.]

lacks some perfection which is its due. For if it is true that the more expert the artisan, the more perfect ⌈and finished⌉ the artifacts produced by his hands, what could ⌈we imagine to⌉ have been produced by this supreme creator of the universe that is not ⌈perfect and⌉ entirely complete in all its parts? Certainly there is no doubt but that God could have created me such that I would never be mistaken; it is also certain that he always wills that which is best. Is it therefore a better thing to ⌈⌐be able to⌐⌉ make a mistake than not to ⌈⌐be able to⌐⌉ do so?

Considering this question with attention, it occurs to me, to begin with, that I should not be astonished at not being able to understand why God does what he does; and that I must not for this reason doubt his existence, since I may perchance observe in my experience many other beings that exist, even though I cannot understand why or how they were made. For, knowing by now that my nature is extremely weak and limited and that God's, on the contrary, is immense, incomprehensible, and infinite, I no longer have any difficulty in recognizing that there are an infinity of things within his power the causes of which lie beyond the powers of my mind. And this consideration alone is sufficient to persuade me that all causes of the type we are accustomed to call final are useless in physical ⌈or natural⌉ affairs, for it does not seem possible for me, without presumption, to seek and undertake to discover the ⌈impenetrable⌉ purposes of God.

Furthermore, it occurs to me that we should not consider a single creation separately when we investigate whether the works of God are perfect, but generally all created objects together. For the same thing which might perhaps, with some sort of justification, appear to be very imperfect if it were alone in the world (56) is seen to be very perfect when considered as constituting a part of this whole universe. And although, since I undertook to doubt everything, I have so far only learned with certainty of my existence and of God's, nevertheless, since I have recognized the infinite power of God, I could not deny that he has produced many other things, or at least that he could produce them, in such a way that I exist and am placed in the world as forming a part of the universality of all beings. [45]

Consequently, when I come to examine myself more closely and to consider what are my errors, which alone testify that there is imperfection in me, I find that they depend upon two joint causes, namely, the faculty of knowing which I possess and the faculty of choice, or rather of free will—that is to say, of my understanding together with my will. For by the understanding alone ⌐I neither assert nor deny anything, but⌐ I only conceive the ideas of things which I may assert or deny. Nor ⌐in considering the understanding thus precisely⌐ can we say that any error is ever found in it, provided that we take the word "error" in its proper sense. And even if there might be in the world an infinity of things of which my understanding has no idea, we cannot therefore say that it is deprived of these ⌐ideas as of something which is owed to its nature⌐, but only that it does not possess them, because in reality there is no argument which can prove that God ought to have given me a greater ⌐and more ample⌐ faculty of knowing than what he has given me; and however adroit ⌐and able⌐ a worker I consider him to be, I must not therefore think that he ought to have put in each of his works all the perfections which he is able to bestow upon some. Thus I cannot complain because God has not given me a sufficiently ample and perfect free will or volition, since ⌐, as a matter of fact,⌐ I experience ⌐it to be so ample and extended⌐ that there are no limits which restrict it.

And it appears to me to be very remarkable that, of all the other qualities which I possess, there is none (57) so perfect or so great that I do not ⌐clearly⌐ recognize that it could be even greater or more perfect. Thus for example, if I consider my faculty of conceiving, I ⌐immediately⌐ recognize that it is of very small extent and greatly limited; and at the same time there occurs to me the idea of another faculty, much more ample, ⟨indeed immensely greater⟩ and even infinite, and from the very fact that I can imagine this I recognize ⌐without diffi-culty⌐ that it belongs to the nature of God. In the same way, if I examine memory, imagination, or any other faculty of mine, I find no one of them which is not quite small and limited and which is not, in God, immense ⌐and infinite⌐. There is only volition alone, ⌐or the liberty of the ⌐free⌐ will,⌐ which I experience to be so great in myself that I cannot con-ceive the idea of any other more ⌐ample and⌐ extended, so that this is what principally indicates to me that I am made in the image and likeness of God. For even though the will may be incomparably greater in God than in myself, either because of the [46] knowledge and the power which are joined with it and which make it surer and more efficacious, or be-cause of its object, since it extends to infinitely more things, nevertheless it does not appear any greater when I consider it formally and precisely by itself. For it consists only in the fact that we can ⌐make a choice; we can⌐ do a given thing or not do it—that is to say, we can affirm or deny, pursue or avoid. Or more properly, our free will consists only in the fact that in affirming or denying, pursuing or avoiding the things sug-gested by the understanding, we behave in such a way that we do not feel that any external force has constrained us in our decision.

For in order to be free, it is not necessary for me to be in-different about the choice of one or the other of the two con-traries, but rather, the more I lean to one, either because I see clearly that it contains ⌐the preponderance (58) of⌐ both goodness and truth or because God so guides my private thoughts, the more freely do I choose ⌐and embrace⌐ it. And certainly, divine grace and natural understanding, far from diminishing my liberty, rather augment and strengthen it. Moreover, that indifference which I feel when I am not more moved toward one side than the other by ⌐the weight of⌐ some reason is the lowest degree of liberty, and is rather a defect in the understanding than a perfection of the will. For if I al-ways understood clearly what is true and what is good, I would never need to deliberate about what judgment and what choice I ought to make, and so I would be entirely free without ever being indifferent.

From all this I recognize, on the one hand, that the cause of my errors is not the power of willing ⟨considered by itself⟩, which I have received from God, for it is very ample and perfect in its own kind. Nor, on the other hand, is it the power of ⌈understanding or⌉ conceiving; for since I conceive nothing except by means of this power which God has given me in order to conceive, no doubt everything I conceive I conceive properly, and it is not possible for me to be deceived in that respect.

Whence, then, do my errors arise? Only from the fact that the will is ⌈much⌉ more ample and far-reaching than the understanding, so that I do not restrain it within the same limits but extend it even to those things which I do not understand. Being ⌈by its nature⌉ indifferent about such matters, it very easily is turned aside from the true and the good ⌈and chooses the false and the evil⌉. And thus it happens that I make mistakes and that I sin.

For example, when I recently examined the question whether anything in the world existed, and I recognized from the very fact that I examined [47] this question that it was very evident that I myself existed, I could not refrain from concluding that what I conceived so clearly was true. Not that I found myself forced to this conclusion by any (59) external cause, but only because the great clarity which was in my understanding produced a great inclination of my will, and I was led to this conviction all the more ⟨spontaneously and⟩ freely as I experienced in myself less indifference. Now, on the contrary, I know not only that I exist, in so far as I am something that thinks, but there is also present in my mind a certain idea of corporeal nature. In consequence, I wonder whether this nature that thinks, which is in me, or rather which is myself, is different from this corporeal nature, or if both are one and the same. I am supposing, here, that I do not yet know any argument to convince me of one possibility

rather than the other, so it follows that I am entirely indifferent as to denying or affirming it, or even as to abstaining from
making any judgment.

And this indifference extends not only to those things with
which the understanding has no acquaintance, but also to all
those generally that it does not comprehend with ⸌sufficient
⸢-ly⸍ perfect⸣ clarity at the moment when the will is deliber-
ating the issue. For however probable may be the conjectures
which incline me to a particular judgment, the mere recognition that they are only conjectures and not certain and indubitable reasons is enough to give me grounds for making
the contrary judgment. I have had sufficient experience of this
in these past few days when I assumed as false all that I had
previously held to be very true, merely because I noticed that
it was somehow possible to doubt it.

Now, if I abstain from making a judgment upon a topic
when I do not conceive it sufficiently clearly and distinctly, it
is evident that I do well and am not making a mistake; but if
I decide to deny or affirm it, then I am not making a proper
use of my free will. And (60) if in this situation I affirm what
is not true, it is evident that I am making a mistake; and even
when I judge according to the truth, it is only by chance, and
I am not for that reason free of blame ⸢for misusing my free-
dom⸣. For the light of nature dictates that the understanding
should always know before the will makes a decision.

It is in this improper use of the free will that we find the
privation which [48] constitutes the essence of error. Privation, I say, is found in the operation in so far as it proceeds
from me, but not in the faculty which I have received from
God, nor even in the operation in so far as it depends upon
him. For certainly I have no reason to complain because God
has not given me a more ample intelligence or a more perfect
insight than what he has bestowed upon me, since it is ⸢actu-
ally⸣ the nature of a finite understanding not to comprehend
many things, and it is the nature of a created understanding
to be finite. On the contrary, far from conceiving such unjust
sentiments as to imagine that he has deprived me or unjustly

kept from me the other perfections with which he has not endowed me, I have every reason to give him thanks because,
never having any obligation to me, he has nevertheless given
me those ⌐few⌐ perfections that I have.

Nor have I any reason to complain because he has given me
a volition more ample than my understanding. For as the
volition consists of just one body, ⌐its subject being⌐ apparently indivisible, it seems that its nature is such that nothing
could be taken from it without destroying it. And, certainly,
the more ample it is, the more reason I have to give thanks
for the generosity of the One who has given it to me.

Nor, finally, have I any reason to complain that God con-
curs with me to perform the acts of this volition, that is, the
judgments in which I am mistaken. For those acts are entirely
true and absolutely good in so far as they depend upon God,
and there is somehow more perfection in my nature because I
can perform them than there would be if I could not. As for
privation, in which alone is found the formal cause (61) of
error and sin, it has no need of any concurrence on the part
of God, since it is not a thing ⌐or a being⌐ and since, if it is
referred to God as to its cause, it should not be called privation but only negation ⌐according to the significance attached
to these words in the schools⌐. For actually it is not an imperfection in God that he has given me the liberty of ⌐judging or
not judging, ⌐or⌐ giving or withholding my assent,ˋ on certain
matters of which he has given me no clear and distinct knowledge. It is, without doubt, an imperfection in myself not to
make proper use of this liberty, and ⌐rashly⌐ to pass judgment
on matters which I ⌐do not rightly understand ⌐and⌐ conceive
only obscurely and confusedly⌐.

I perceive, nevertheless, that it would have been easy for
God to contrive that I would never make mistakes, even
though I remained free and with limited knowledge. He
might, for example, have given my understanding [49] a clear
and distinct comprehension of all the things about which I
should ever deliberate, or he might simply have engraved so
deeply in my memory the resolution never to pass judgment

on anything without conceiving it clearly and distinctly that
I could never forget this rule. And I ⸢readily⸣ recognize ⸢in so
far as I possess the comprehension of any whole,⸣ that ⸢when I
consider myself alone, as if I were the only person in the
world,⸣ I would have been ⸢much⸣ more perfect than I am if
God had so created me ⸢that I never made a mistake⸣; nevertheless I cannot therefore deny that the universe may be somehow more perfect because some of its parts are not free from
defect ⸢while others are⸣, than it would be if all its parts were
alike.

And I have no right to complain because God, having put
me in the world, has not wished to place me in the ranks of
the noblest and most perfect beings. ⸢I indeed have reason to
rejoice because,⸣ even if I do not have the power of avoiding
error by the first method ⸢which I have just described⸣, which
depends upon a clear and evident knowledge of all the things
about which I can deliberate, the other method, at least, is
within my power. This is, (62) firmly to adhere to the resolution never to pass judgment upon things whose truth is not
clearly known to me. For even though I experience in myself
the weakness of not being able to keep my mind continuously
faithful to a fixed resolution, I can nevertheless, by attentive
and frequently repeated meditation, so strongly impress it
upon my memory that I will never fail to recollect it whenever there is need, and thus I can acquire the habit of not
erring. And since this comprises the greatest and principal
perfection of man, I consider that I have benefited not a little
by today's meditation, in having discovered the cause of error
and falsity.

And certainly, there can be no other cause than the one I
have just explained, for whenever I restrict my volition within
the bounds of my knowledge, whenever my volition makes no
judgment except upon matters clearly and distinctly reported
to it by the understanding, it cannot happen that I err. For
every clear and distinct conception is without doubt something ⸢real and positive⸣, and thus cannot derive its origin
from nothingness, but must have God for its author—God, I

say, who, [50] being supremely perfect, cannot be the cause of any error—and consequently we must conclude that such a conception ⌈or such a judgment⌉ is true.

For the rest, I have not only learned today what I must avoid in order not to err, but also what I ought to do to arrive at the knowledge of the truth. For I shall certainly achieve this goal if I hold my attention sufficiently fixed upon all those things which I conceive perfectly and if I distinguish these from the others which I conceive only confusedly and obscurely. And from now on I shall take particular care to act accordingly. (63)

FIFTH MEDITATION

OF THE ESSENCE OF MATERIAL THINGS AND, ONCE MORE, OF GOD: THAT HE EXISTS

There are many other questions for me to inquire into concerning the attributes of God and concerning my own nature, or the nature of my mind. I may, perhaps, pursue this investigation some other time; for the present, having noticed what must be done or avoided in order to arrive at the knowledge of the truth, my principal task is to attempt to escape from ⌈and relieve myself of all⌉ the doubts into which I have fallen in these last few days, and to see if we cannot know anything certain about material objects. But before examining whether such objects exist outside of myself, I must consider the concepts of these objects, in so far as they occur in my thought, and see which of them are distinct and which of them are confused.

In the first place, I picture distinctly that quantity which philosophers commonly call the "continuum," or extension in length, width, and depth which exists in this quantity, or rather in the body to which we attribute it. Furthermore, I can distinguish in it various different parts and attribute to each of these parts all sorts of sizes, shapes, positions, and movements; and, finally, I can assign to each of these movements all degrees of duration.

And I not only know these things distinctly when I consider them thus in general, but also, ⌐however little I am⌐ applying my attention to it, I ⌐⸜come to⸝⌐ recognize an infinity of details concerning [51] numbers, shapes, movements, and other similar things, the truth of which makes itself so apparent (64) and accords so well with my nature that when I discover them for the first time it does not seem ⌐to me⌐ as though I were learning anything new, but rather as though I were remembering what I had previously known—that is, that I am perceiving things which were already in my mind, even though I had not yet focussed my attention upon them.

And what I believe to be more important here is that I find in myself an infinity of ideas of certain things which cannot be assumed to be pure nothingness, even though they may perhaps have no existence outside of my thought. These things are not figments of my imagination, even though it is within my power to think of them or not to think of them; on the contrary, they have their own true and immutable natures. Thus, for example, when I imagine a triangle, even though there may perhaps be no such figure anywhere in the world outside of my thought, nor ever have been, nevertheless the figure cannot help having a certain determinate nature, or form, or essence, which is immutable and eternal, which I have not invented and which does not in any way depend upon my mind. This is evidenced by the fact that we can demonstrate various properties of this triangle, namely, that its three angles are equal to two right angles, that the greatest angle subtends the longest side, and other similar properties. Whether I wish it or not, I ⸜now⸝ recognize ⌐very⌐ clearly ⌐and evidently⌐ that these are properties of the triangle, even though I had never previously thought of them in any way when I first imagined one. And therefore it cannot be said that I have ⌐imagined or⌐ invented them.

Nor can I raise the objection here that possibly this idea of the triangle came to my mind ⌐from external things⌐ through the medium of my senses, since I have sometimes seen triangularly shaped objects; for I can picture in my mind an infinity of other shapes such that I cannot have the least suspicion that they have ever been present to my senses, and I am still (65) no less able to demonstrate various properties about their nature than I am about that of the triangle. These properties, certainly, must be wholly true, since I conceive them clearly. And thus they are something, and not pure negation, since it is quite evident that everything which is true is something ⌐, as truth is the same as being⌐. I have already amply demonstrated that everything that I recognize clearly and [52] distinctly is true; and even if I had not demonstrated this, the nature of my mind is such that I can ⌐nevertheless⌐ not help believing things to be true while I am conceiving them clearly ⌐and distinctly⌐. And I recollect that even when I was still strongly attached to the objects of sense, I numbered among the most constant truths that which I conceived clearly ⌐and distinctly⌐ about the shapes, numbers, and other properties which belong to the fields of arithmetic and geometry ⌐or, in general, to pure and abstract mathematics⌐.

Now, if from the very fact that I can derive from my thoughts the idea of something, it follows that all that I clearly and distinctly recognize as characteristic of this thing does in reality characterize it, can I not derive from this an argument which will ⌐demonstratively⌐ prove the existence of God? It is certain that I find in my mind the idea of God, of a supremely perfect Being, no less than that of any shape or number whatsoever; and I recognize that an ⌐actual and⌐ eternal existence belongs to his nature no less clearly and distinctly than I recognize that all I can demonstrate about some figure or number actually belongs to the nature of that figure or number. Thus, even if everything that I concluded in the preceding Meditations were ⌐by chance⌐ not true, the existence of God should pass in my mind as at least as certain (66) as I have hitherto considered all the truths of mathematics ⌐, which deal only with numbers and figures¬.

And this is true even though I must admit that it does not at first appear entirely obvious, but seems to have some appearance of sophistry. For since in all other matters I have become accustomed to make a distinction between existence and essence, I am easily convinced that the existence of God can be separated from his essence, and that thus I can conceive of God as not actually existing. Nevertheless, when I consider this with more attention, I find it manifest that we can no more separate the existence of God from his essence than we can separate from the essence of a ⌐rectilinear¬ triangle the fact that the size of its three angles equals two right angles, or from the idea of a mountain the idea of a valley. Thus it is no less self-contradictory to conceive of a God, a supremely perfect Being, who lacks existence—that is, who lacks some perfection—than it is to conceive of a mountain for which there is no valley.

But even though in fact I cannot conceive of a God without existence, any more than of a mountain without a valley, nevertheless, just as from the mere fact that I conceive a mountain with a valley, it does not [53] follow that any mountain exists in the world, so likewise, though I conceive of God as existing, it does not seem to follow for this reason that God exists. For my thought does not impose any necessity upon things; and just as I can at my pleasure imagine a winged horse, even though no horse has wings, so I could perhaps attribute existence to God, even though no God existed.

⌐This is far from the truth;¬ it is here that there is sophistry hidden ⌐under the guise of a valid objection¬. For from the fact that I cannot conceive a mountain without a valley it does not follow that there is a mountain or a valley anywhere ⌐in the world¬, but only that the mountain (67) and the valley, whether they exist or not, are inseparable from each other. From the fact alone that I cannot conceive God except as existing, it follows that existence is inseparable from him, and consequently that he does, in truth, exist. Not that my thought can bring about this result or that it imposes any necessity upon things; on the contrary, the necessity which is in the thing itself—that is, the necessity of the existence of God—determines me to have this thought. For it is not in my power to conceive of a God without existence—that is to say, of a supremely perfect Being without a supreme perfection—as it is in my power to imagine a horse either with or without wings.

And it must not be said here that it is only necessary that I admit that God exists after I have supposed that he possesses all sorts of perfections, since existence is one of them, but that my first supposition was not really necessary. Thus it is not necessary to think that all four-sided figures can be inscribed in a circle; but if we suppose that I do have this idea, I am forced to admit that a rhombus can be inscribed in one, ⌜since it is a four-sided figure,⌝ and ⌜by⌝ this ⌜I will be forced to admit what⌝ is ⟨clearly⟩ false. We must not, I say, argue thus; for even though it is not necessary that I should ever have any thought about God, nevertheless, whenever I do choose to think of a first and supreme being and to derive ⌜, so to speak,⌝ the idea of God from the treasure house of my mind, it is necessary that I attribute to him all kinds of perfections, even though it does not occur to me to mention them all and to pay attention to each one of them severally. And this necessity is enough to bring it about that afterward, as soon as I come to recognize that existence is a perfection, I conclude ⟨very properly⟩ that this first and supreme Being ⌜truly⌝ exists; just as it is not necessary that I should ever imagine any triangle, but [54] every time that I wish to consider a rectilinear figure containing three angles only, it is absolutely necessary that I attribute to it everything that leads (68) to the conclusion that these three angles are not greater than two right angles, even if perhaps I do not then consider this matter in particular. But when I wish to determine what figures can be inscribed in a circle, it is in no way necessary that I think that all four-sided figures are of this number; on the contrary, I cannot even pretend that this is the case as long as I do not wish to accept anything but what I can conceive clearly and distinctly. Consequently, there is a vast difference between false suppositions, such as this one, and the true ideas which are inborn in me, of which the first and chief one is that of God. For actually I have several reasons for recognizing that this idea is not something ⌐imaginary or⌐ fictitious, depending only on my thought, but that it is the image of a true and immutable nature. The first reason is that I cannot conceive anything but God alone, to whose essence existence belongs ⌐with necessity⌐. Another reason is that it is not possible for me to conceive ⌐in the same way⌐ two or more gods ⌐such as he⌐. Again, assuming that there is now a God who exists, I see clearly that he must have existed before from all eternity and that he should be eternally in the future. And a final reason is that I conceive various other qualities in God, of which I can neither diminish nor change a particle.

For the rest, whatever proof or argument I use, I must always come back to this conclusion: that it is only the things that I conceive clearly and distinctly which have the power to convince me completely. And although among the things which I conceive in this way there are, in truth, some which are obvious ⌐-ly known⌐ to everyone, while others of them only become known to those who consider them more closely and examine them more carefully, nevertheless, after they have once been discovered, none of them can be esteemed less certain than the rest. Thus, for example, in every right-angled triangle, even though it is not so readily apparent (69) that the square of the hypotenuse is equal to the squares of the other two sides as it is that this hypotenuse is opposite the greatest angle, nevertheless, after this fact has once been recognized, we are as much convinced of the truth of the one proposition as of the other. And as for the question of God, certainly, if my mind were not prejudiced and if my thought were not distracted by the ⌐constant⌐ presence ⌐on all sides⌐ of images of sensible objects, [55] there would be nothing that I would recognize sooner or more easily than God. For is there anything ⌈clearer and⌉ more obvious in itself than ⌈to think⌉ that there is a God, ⌈that is to say,⌉ a supreme ⌈and perfect⌉ Being, in whom ⟨uniquely⟩ ⌈necessary or eternal⌉ existence is included in essence, and who consequently exists?

And although, in order thoroughly to understand this truth, I have had to make a great mental effort, nevertheless I find myself at present not only as certain of this as of everything which seems to me most certain, but even beyond that I notice that the certainty of all other things depends upon this so ⌈absolutely⌉ that, without this knowledge, it is impossible ever to be able to know anything perfectly.

For even though my nature is such that as soon as I understand anything very clearly and very distinctly I cannot help but believe it to be true, nevertheless, because I am also of such a nature that I cannot always confine my attention to one thing and frequently remember having judged a thing to be true when I have ceased considering the reasons which forced me to that conclusion, it can happen at such a time that other reasons occur to me which would easily make me change my mind if I did not know that there was a God. And so I would never have true and certain knowledge concerning anything at all, but only vague and fluctuating opinions.

Thus, for example, when I consider the nature of the ⌈⟨rectilinear⟩⌉ triangle, I recognize ⟨most⟩ evidently, I, who am somewhat skilled in geometry, that its three angles are equal to two right angles; nor can I disbelieve this while I am paying attention to (70) its demonstration. But as soon as I turn my attention away from the demonstration, even while I remember having clearly understood it, it can easily happen that I doubt its truth, if I do not know that there is a God. For I can persuade myself that I was so made by nature that I could easily make mistakes, even in those matters which I believe I understand with the greatest evidence ⌈and certainty⌉, especially because I remember having often judged many things true and certain, which, later, other reasons constrained me to consider absolutely false.

But after having recognized that there is a God, and having recognized at the same time that all things are dependent upon him and that he is not a deceiver, I can infer as a consequence that everything which I conceive clearly and distinctly is necessarily true. Therefore, even if I am no longer thinking of the reasons why [56] I have judged something to be true, provided only I remember having understood it clearly and distinctly, there can never be a reason on the other side which can make me consider the matter doubtful. Thus I have ⌐a¬ true and certain ⌐body of¬ knowledge ⌐on this matter⌐. And this same ⌐body of¬ knowledge extends also to all the other things which I remember having formerly demonstrated, such as the truths of geometry and other similar matters. For what reason can anyone give to make me doubt them? Would it be that my nature is such that I am ⌐very likely to be¬ ⌐frequently⌐ deceived? But I know already that I cannot go wrong in judgments for which I clearly know the reasons. Would it be that I have formerly considered many things true and certain which I later recognized to be false? But I had not clearly or distinctly known any of those things; and not yet knowing this rule by which I am certain of truth, I had been led to believe them by reasons that I have since recognized to be less strong than I had then imagined them. What further objections could be raised? Would it be that possibly I am asleep, as I had myself argued earlier, or that all the thoughts that I now have are no more true than the dreams we imagine when asleep? But ⌐even so, nothing would be altered. For⌐ (71) even if I were asleep, all that appears evident to my mind is absolutely true.

And thus I recognize very clearly that the certainty and truth of all knowledge depends solely on the knowledge of the true God, so that before I knew him I could not know any other thing perfectly. And now that I know him, I have the means of acquiring ⌐clear and certain ⌐and⌐ perfect⌐ knowledge about an infinity of things, not only about God himself ⌐and about other intellectual matters⌐, but also about ⌐that which pertains to⌐ corporeal nature, in so far as it can be the object of ⌐pure mathematics ⌐—that is, of\ the demonstrations of geometricians who are not concerned with its existence⌐. [57]

SIXTH MEDITATION

OF THE EXISTENCE OF CORPOREAL THINGS AND OF THE REAL DISTINCTION BETWEEN THE MIND AND BODY ⌐OF MAN⌐

Nothing more is now left for me to do except to examine whether corporeal things exist; and I already know ⌐for certain⌐ that they can exist at least in so far as they are considered as the objects ⌐of pure mathematics, ⌐or\ of the demonstrations of geometry,⌐ since I conceive them in this way very clearly and very distinctly. For there is no doubt but that God has the power of producing everything that I am able to conceive with distinctness; and I have never supposed that it was impossible for him to do anything, except only when I found a contradiction in being able to conceive it well. Furthermore, my faculty of imagination, which I find by experience that I use when I apply myself to the consideration of material objects, is capable of persuading me of their existence. For when I consider attentively what the imagination is, (72) I find that it is nothing else than a particular application of the faculty of knowledge to a body which is intimately present to it and which therefore exists.

And to make this ⌐very⌐ obvious, I take note of the difference between imagination and pure intellection ⌐or conception⌐. For example, when I imagine a triangle, not only do I conceive that it is a figure composed of three lines, but along with that I envision these three lines as present, by the force ⌐and the internal effort⌐ of my mind; and it is just this that I call "imagination." But if I wish to think of a chiliogon, I recognize quite well, indeed, that it is a figure composed of a thousand sides, as easily as I conceive that a triangle is a figure composed of ⌐only¬ three sides, but I cannot imagine the thousand sides ⌐of a chiliogon as I can the three of a triangle, nor, so to speak, look at them¬ as though they were present ⌐to the eyes of my mind¬. And although, following my habit of always using my imagination when I think of corporeal things, it may happen that in conceiving a chiliogon I confusedly picture some figure to myself, nevertheless it is ⌐quite¬ evident that this figure is not a chiliogon, since it is in no way different from what I would picture to myself if I thought of a myriogon or of some other figure of many sides, and that it in no way serves [58] to bring out the properties which constitute the difference between the chiliogon and the other polygons. But if it is a question of considering a pentagon, ⌐it is quite true that¬ I can conceive its shape, just as well as that of a chiliogon, without the aid of the imagination; but I can also imagine it by applying my mind attentively to each of its five sides, and ⌐at the same time⌐ ⌐collectively¬ to the area ⌐or space¬ that they enclose.

Thus I recognize clearly that I have need of a special (73) mental effort in order to imagine, which I do not require in order to ⌐conceive ⌐or¬ understand⌐, and this ⌐special¬ mental effort clearly shows the difference that exists between imagination and pure intellection ⌐or conception¬. In addition, I notice that this ability to imagine which I possess, in so far as it differs from the power of conceiving, is in no way necessary to my ⌐nature or¬ essence, that is to say, to the essence of my mind. For even if I did not possess it, there is no doubt that I would still remain the same person I now am, from which it seems to follow that it depends upon something other than my mind. And I readily conceive that if some body exists with which my mind is so joined ⌐and united¬ that it can consider it whenever it wishes, it could be that by this means it imagines corporeal things. Thus this method of thinking only differs from pure intellection in that the mind, in conceiving, turns somehow toward itself and considers some one of the ideas which it possesses in itself, whereas in imagining it turns toward the body and considers in the latter something conformable to the idea which it has either thought of by itself or perceived through the senses. I easily conceive, I say, that the imagination can work in this fashion, if it is true that there are bodies; and because I cannot find any other way in which this can be explained ⟨equally well⟩, I therefore conjecture that bodies probably exist. But this is only a probability; and although I carefully consider all aspects of the question, I nevertheless do not see that from this distinct idea of corporeal nature which I find in my imagination, I can derive any argument which necessarily proves the existence of any body. (74)

But I have become accustomed to imagine many other things besides that corporeal nature which is the object of ⟨pure mathematics ⌈or⟩ geometry⌉, although less distinctly, such as colors, sounds, tastes, pain, and other similar qualities. And inasmuch as I perceive those qualities much better by the senses, through the medium of which, with the help of the memory, they seem to have reached my imagination, [59] I believe that in order to examine them more readily it is appropriate to consider at the same time the nature of the sensation and to see whether, from those ideas which are perceived by the method of thinking which I call "sensation," I will not be able to derive some certain proof of the existence of corporeal things.

First, I shall recall in my memory what are the things which I formerly held to be true because I had received them through the senses, and what were the bases on which my belief was founded. Afterward I shall examine the reasons which since then have obliged me to consider them doubtful, and finally, I shall consider what I ought now to believe ⟨about them⟩.

First, then, I felt that I had a head, hands, feet, and ⌈all the⌉ other members which compose this body which I thought of as a part, or possibly even as the whole, of myself. Furthermore, I felt that this body was one of a world of bodies, from

which it was capable of receiving various advantages and disadvantages; and I identified these advantages by a certain feeling of pleasure ⌈or enjoyment⌉, and the disadvantages by a
feeling of pain. Besides this pleasure and pain, I also experienced hunger, thirst, and other similar appetites, as well as
certain bodily tendencies toward gaiety, sadness, anger, and
other similar emotions. And externally, in addition to the extension, shapes, and (75) movements of bodies, I observed in
them hardness, warmth, and ⌈all the⌉ other qualities perceived
by touch. Furthermore, I noticed in them light, colors, odors,
tastes, and sounds, the variety of which enabled me to distinguish the sky, the earth, the sea, and ⌈, in general, all⌉ other
bodies, one from another.

And certainly, considering the ideas of all these qualities
which were presented to my mind [1] and which alone I directly
sensed, in the true significance of that term, it was not without reason that I believed I had sensory knowledge of things
entirely different from my thought—of bodies, namely, from
which these ideas came. For I was aware that these ideas occurred without the necessity of my consent, so that I could
not perceive any object, however much I wished, unless it was
present to one of my sense organs; nor was it in my power
not to perceive it when it was present. [60] And because the
ideas I received through the senses were much more vivid,
more detailed, and even in their own way more distinct than
any of those which I could picture to myself ⌐with conscious
purpose⌐ while meditating, or even than those which I found
impressed upon my memory, it seemed that they could not be
derived from my own mind, and therefore they must have
been produced in me by some other things. Of these things I
have no knowledge ⌐whatsoever,⌐ except that derived from the
ideas themselves, so nothing else could occur to my mind except that those things were similar to the ideas they caused.
And since I remembered that I had used my senses earlier
than my reason, and since I recognized that the ideas I formed
by myself were not as detailed as those I received through the

---

[1] [L. cogitatio; F. pensée.]

senses and were most commonly composed of the latter as parts, I easily became persuaded that I had no idea in my mind which I had not previously acquired through my senses.

It was also not without reason that I believed that this body, which by a certain particular privilege I called mine, (76) belonged to me more ⌜properly and strictly⌝ than any other. For in fact I could never be separated from it, as I could be from other bodies; I felt in it and for it all my appetites and all my emotions; and finally I experienced ⌜the sensations of⌝ pain and ⌜the thrill of⌝ pleasure in its parts, and not in those of other bodies which are separated from it.

But when I inquired why any particular sensation of pain should be followed by unhappiness in the mind and the thrill of pleasure should give rise to happiness, or even why a particular feeling of the stomach, which I call hunger, makes us want to eat, and the dryness of the throat makes us want to drink, and so on, I could give no reason except that nature teaches me so. For there is certainly no affinity ⌜and no relationship⌝, or at least none that I ⌜can⌝ understand, between the feeling in the stomach and the desire to eat, no more than between the perception of the object which causes pain and the feeling of displeasure produced by it. And in the same way, it seemed to me that I had learned from nature all the other beliefs which I held about the objects of my senses, since I noticed that the judgments I habitually made about these objects took form in my mind before I had the opportunity to weigh ⌜and consider⌝ any reasons which could oblige me to make them. [61]

Later on, various experiences gradually destroyed all my faith in my senses. For I often observed that towers which, viewed from far away, had appeared round to me, seemed at close range to be square, and that colossal statues placed on the highest summits of these towers appeared small when viewed from below. And similarly in a multitude of other experiences, I encountered errors in judgments based on the external senses. And not only on the external senses, but even on the internal ones, (77) for is there anything more intimate

⌐or more internal⌐ than pain? Yet I have learned from certain persons whose arms or legs had been amputated that it still seemed to them sometimes that they felt pain in the parts which they no longer possessed. This gives me reason to think that I could not be ⌐entirely⌐ sure either that there was something wrong with one of my limbs, even though I felt a pain in it.

And to these reasons for doubting I have recently added two other very general ones. The first is that I have never thought I perceived anything when awake that I might not sometimes also think I perceived when I am asleep; and since I do not believe that the things I seem to perceive when asleep proceed from objects outside of myself, I did not see any better reason why I ought to believe this about what I seem to perceive when awake. The other reason was that, not yet knowing, or rather pretending not to know the author of my being, I saw nothing to make it impossible that I was so constructed by nature that I should be mistaken even in the things which seemed to me most true.

And as for the reasons which had previously persuaded me that sensible objects truly existed, I did not find it very difficult to answer them. For as nature seemed to lead me to many conclusions from which reason dissuaded me, I did not believe that I ought to have much faith in the teachings of this nature. And although my sense perceptions do not depend upon my volition, I did not think that I should therefore conclude that they proceeded from things different from myself, since there might perhaps be some faculty in myself even though it has been thus far unknown to me, which could ⌐be their cause and⌐ produce them.

But now that I am beginning to know myself better and to discover more clearly the author of my origin, I do not think in truth that I ought rashly to admit everything which the senses seem to teach us, (78) but on the other hand I do not think that I should doubt them all in general. [62]

First, since I know that all the things I conceive [2] clearly

_____

2 [L. *intelligo;* F. *concevoir.*]

and distinctly can be produced by God exactly as I conceive them, it is sufficient that I can clearly and distinctly conceive one thing apart from another to be certain that the one is distinct ⌈or different⌉ from the other. For they can be made to exist separately, at least by ⌈the omnipotence of⌉ God, and we are obliged to consider them different no matter what power produces this separation. From the very fact that I know with certainty that I exist, and that I find that ⟨absolutely⟩ nothing else belongs ⌈necessarily⌉ to my nature or essence except that I am a thinking being, I readily conclude that my essence consists solely in being a body which thinks ⌈or a substance whose whole essence or nature is only to think⌉. And although perhaps, or rather certainly, as I will soon show, I have a body with which I am very closely united, nevertheless, since on the one hand I have a clear and distinct idea of myself in so far as I am only a thinking and not an extended being, and since on the other hand I have a distinct idea of body in so far as it is only an extended being which does not think, it is certain that this "I" ⌈—that is to say, my soul, by virtue of which I am what I am—⌉ is entirely ⌈and truly⌉ distinct from my body and that it can ⌈be or⌉ exist without it.

Furthermore, I find in myself various faculties of thinking which each have their own particular characteristics ⌈and are distinct from myself⌉. For example, I find in myself the faculties of imagination and of perception, without which I might no doubt conceive of myself, clearly and distinctly, as a whole being; but I could not ⟨, conversely,⟩ conceive of those faculties without me, that is to say, without an intelligent substance ⌈to which they are attached ⟨or⟩ in which they inhere⟩. For ⌈in our notion of them or, to use the scholastic vocabulary,⌉ in their formal concept, they embrace some type of intellection. From all this I reach the conception that these faculties are distinct from me as ⌈shapes, movements, and other⌉ modes ⌈or accidents of objects⌉ are distinct from ⌈the very⌉ objects ⌈that sustain them⌉.

I also recognize ⌈in myself⌉ some other faculties, such as the power of changing location, of assuming various postures, and

other similar ones; which cannot be conceived without some
substance in which they inhere, any more than the preceding
ones, (79) and which therefore cannot exist without such a
substance. But it is ⌜quite⌝ evident that these faculties, if
⌜it is true that⌝ they exist, must inhere in some corporeal or
extended substance, and not in an intelligent substance, since
their clear and distinct concept does actually involve some
sort of extension, but no sort of intelligence whatsoever. [63]
Furthermore, ⌜⸝I cannot doubt that⸜⌝ there is in me a certain
passive faculty of perceiving, that is, of receiving and recognizing the ideas of sensible objects; but ⌜it would be valueless
to me, and⌝ I could in no way use it if there were not ⸝also⸜
in me, or in something else, another active faculty capable of
forming and producing these ideas. But this active faculty
cannot be in me ⌜, in so far as I am a thinking being⌝, since it
does not at all presuppose ⌜my⌝ intelligence and also since
those ideas often occur to me without my contributing to
them in any way, and even ⸝frequently⸜ against my will. Thus
it must necessarily exist in some substance different from myself, in which all the reality that exists objectively in the
ideas produced by this faculty is formally or eminently contained, as I have said before. This substance is either a body—
that is, a corporeal nature—in which is formally ⌜and actually⌝
contained all that which is contained objectively ⌜and by rep-
resentation⌝ in these ideas; or else it is God himself, or some
other creation more noble than the body, in which all this is
eminently contained.

But since God is not a deceiver, it is very manifest that he
does not send me these ideas directly by his own agency, nor
by the mediation of some creation in which their ⸝objective⸜
reality does not exist formally but only eminently. For since
he has not given me any faculty for recognizing what that creation might be, but on the contrary a very great (80) inclination to believe that these ideas come from corporeal objects, I
do not see how we could clear God of the charge of deceit if
these ideas did in fact come from some other source ⌜or were
produced by other causes⌝ than corporeal objects. Therefore

we must conclude that corporeal objects exist. Nevertheless, they are not perhaps entirely what our senses perceive them to be, for there are many ways in which this sense perception is very obscure and confused; but ⌐we must⌐ at least ⌐admit that⌐ everything which I conceive clearly and distinctly ⌐⌐as occurring⌐ in them—that is to say, everything, generally speaking, which is discussed in pure ⌐mathematics ⌐or⌐ geometry⌐—does in truth occur in them.

⌐As for the rest,⌐ there are other beliefs, which are very doubtful and uncertain, which are either merely particular— as, for example, that the sun is of such a size and such a shape —or else are conceived less clearly ⌐and less distinctly⌐—such as light, sound, pain, and other similar things. Nevertheless, from the mere fact that God is not [64] a deceiver, and that in consequence he has not permitted any falsity in my opinions without having given me some faculty capable of correcting it, ⌐I think I can conclude with assurance that⌐ I have ⌐some hope of learning the truth even about these matters ⌐and⌐ the means of knowing them with certainty⌐.

First, there is no doubt but that all that nature teaches me contains some truth. For by nature, considered in general, I now understand nothing else but God himself, or else the ⌐order and⌐ system that God has established for created things; and by my nature in particular I understand nothing else but the arrangement ⌐or assemblage⌐ of all that God has given me.

Now there is nothing that this nature teaches me more expressly ⌐or more obviously⌐ than that I have a body which is in poor condition when I feel pain, which needs food or drink when I have the feelings of hunger or thirst, and so on. And therefore I ought to have no doubt that in this there is some truth. (81)

Nature also teaches me by these feelings of pain, hunger, thirst, and so on that I am not only residing in my body, as a pilot in his ship, but furthermore, that I am intimately connected with it, and that ⌐the mixture is⌐ so blended ⌐, as it were,⌐ that ⌐something like⌐ a single whole is produced. For if that were not the case, when my body is wounded I would not therefore feel pain, I, who am only a thinking being; but I would perceive that wound by the understanding alone, as a pilot perceives by sight if something in his vessel is broken. And when my body needs food or drink, I would simply know the fact itself, instead of ⌐receiving notice of it by⌐ having confused feelings of hunger and thirst. For actually all these feelings of hunger, thirst, pain, and so on are nothing else but certain confused modes of thinking, which have their origin in ⌐and depend upon⌐ the union and apparent fusion of the mind with the body.

Furthermore, nature teaches me that many other bodies exist in the vicinity of my own, of which I must seek some and avoid others. And certainly, from the fact that I perceive different kinds of colors, odors, tastes, sounds, heat, hardness, and so on, I very readily conclude that in the objects from which these various sense perceptions proceed there are some corresponding variations, although perhaps these variations are not really similar to the perceptions. And from the fact that some of these ⌐various sense⌐ perceptions are agreeable to me and others are disagreeable, [65] there is absolutely no doubt that my body, or rather my whole self, in so far as I am composed of body and mind, can in various ways be benefited or harmed by the other objects which surround it. (82)

But there are many other opinions that nature has apparently taught me which, however, I have not truly learned from her, but which were introduced into my mind by my habit of judging things inattentively. Thus it can easily happen that these opinions contain some falsity—as, for example, my opinion that all spaces in which there is nothing which ⌐affects and⌐ makes an impression on my senses are empty; that in an object which is hot there is some quality similar to my idea of heat; that in a white, ⌐or black,⌐ ⟨or green⟩ object there is the same whiteness, ⌐or blackness,⌐ ⟨or greenness⟩ that I perceive; that in a bitter or sweet object there is the same taste ⌐or the same flavor⌐, and so on for the other senses; and that stars, towers, and all other distant objects are the same shape and size that they appear ⌐from afar⌐ to our eyes, and so forth.

In order that there should be nothing in this matter that I do not conceive ⟨sufficiently⟩ distinctly, I should define ⟨more⟩ precisely what I properly mean when I say that nature teaches me something. For I am here using the word "nature" in a more restricted sense than when I use it to mean a combination ⌐or assemblage¬ of everything God has given me, seeing that this ⌐assemblage or¬ combination includes many things which pertain to the mind alone, to which I do not intend to refer here when speaking of nature—as ⌐for example¬ my knowledge ⌐of this truth:¬ that what has ⌐once¬ been done can never ⌐after¬ not have been done, and ⟨all ⌐of⟩ an infinity of¬ other ⌐similar¬ truths known to me by the light of nature ⌐without any aid of the body¬. Such an assemblage also includes many other things which belong to body alone and are not here included under the name of "nature," such as its quality of being heavy and many other similar ones; for I am not concerned with these either, but only with those things which God has presented to me as a being composed of mind and body. This nature effectively teaches me to avoid things which produce in me the feeling of pain and to seek those which make me have some feeling of pleasure ⟨and so on⟩. But I do not see that beyond this it teaches me that I should ever conclude anything from these various sense perceptions concerning things outside of ourselves, unless the mind has ⌐carefully and¬ maturely examined them. For it seems to me that it is the business of the mind alone, and not [66] of the being composed of mind and body, to decide the truth of such matters. (83)

Thus, although a star makes no more impression on my eye than the flame of a candle, and there is no real ⟨or positive inclination⟩ ⌐or natural faculty¬ in me that leads me to believe that it is larger than this flame, nevertheless I have so judged it from infancy for no adequate reason. And although in approaching the flame I feel heat, and even though in approaching it a little too closely I feel pain, there is still no reason that can convince me that there is some quality in the flame similar to this heat, any more than to this pain. I only have reason to believe there is some quality in it, whatever it may be, which arouses in me these feelings of heat or pain.

Similarly, although there are parts of space in which I find nothing that ⌈excites and⌉ affects my senses, I ought not therefore to conclude that they contain no objects. Thus I see that both here and in many other similar cases I am accustomed to ⌈misunderstand and⌉ misconstrue the order of nature, because although these ⌈sensations or⌉ sense perceptions were given to me only to indicate to my mind which objects are useful or harmful to the composite body of which it is a part, and are for that purpose sufficiently clear and distinct, I nevertheless use them as though they were very certain rules by which I could obtain direct information about the essence ⌈and the nature⌉ of external objects, about which they can of course give me no information except very obscurely and confusedly.

In the previous discussion I have already explained sufficiently how it happens, despite the supreme goodness of God, that error occurs in my judgments. One further difficulty, though, presents itself here. This concerns objects which I am taught by nature to seek or avoid and also the internal sensations which she has given me. For it seems to me that I have noticed error here ⌈and thus that I am sometimes directly deceived by my nature⌉—as, for example, when the pleasant taste of some food in which poison has been mixed can induce me to take the poison, and so misleads me. (84) It is nevertheless true that in this case nature ⌈can be excused, for it⌉ only leads me to desire the food in which a pleasant taste is found, and not [67] to desire the poison which is unknown to it. Thus I cannot conclude anything from this except that my nature is not entirely and universally cognizant of all things. And at this there is no reason to be surprised, since man, being of a finite nature, is also restricted to a knowledge of a limited perfection.

But we also make mistakes sufficiently frequently even about matters of which we are directly informed by nature, as happens to sick people when they desire to drink or eat things which ⌈can⌉ ⟨later⟩ harm them. It might be argued here that the reason that they err is that their nature is corrupted. But this does not remove the difficulty, for a sick man is in truth no less the creation of God than is a man in full health, and therefore it is just as inconsistent with the goodness of God for him as for the other to have a ⌈misleading and⌉ faulty nature. A clock, composed of wheels and counterweights, is no less exactly obeying all the laws of nature when it is badly made and does not mark the time correctly than when it completely fulfills the intention of its maker; so also, the human body may be considered as a machine, so built and composed of bones, nerves, muscles, veins, blood, and skin that even if there were no mind in it, it would not cease to move in all the ways that it does at present when it is not moved under the direction of the will, nor consequently with the aid of the mind ⌈, but only by the condition of its organs⌉. I readily recognize that it is quite natural, for example, for this body to suffer dryness in the throat as a result of a dropsical condition, and thus to produce a feeling of thirst in the mind and a consequent disposition on the part of the mind to stimulate the nerves and other parts in the manner requisite for drinking, and so to increase the body's illness ⌈and injure itself⌉. It is just as natural, I say, as it is for it to be beneficially influenced to drink by a similar dryness of the throat, when it is not ill at all. (85)

And although in considering the purpose for which a clock has been intended by its designer, I can say that it is false to its nature when it does not correctly indicate the time, and although in considering the mechanism of the human body in the same way as having been formed ⌈by God⌉ to provide all the customary activities, I have reason to think that it is not functioning according to its nature when its throat is dry and drinking injures its chances of self-preservation, I nevertheless recognize that this last usage of the word "nature" is very different from the other. For the latter is nothing else but an arbitrary appellation [68] which depends entirely on my own idea in comparing a sick man and a poorly made clock, and contrasting them with my idea of a healthy man and a well-made clock; this appellation refers to nothing which is actually found in the objects of which we are talking. On the contrary, by the other usage of the word "nature," I mean something which is actually found in objects and which therefore is not without some truth.

But certainly, although as far as a dropsical body is concerned, it is only an arbitrary appellation to say that its nature is corrupted when, without needing to drink, it still has a dry and arid throat; nevertheless, when we consider the composite body ⌜as a whole⌝—that is to say, the mind ⌜or soul⌝ united with the body—it is not a pure appellation, but ⌜truly⌝ an actual error on the part of nature that it is thirsty when it is very harmful to it to drink. Therefore we must examine how it is that the goodness of God does not prevent man's nature, so considered, from being faulty ⌜and deceptive⌝.

⌜To begin this examination,⌝ I first take notice here that there is a great difference between the mind and the body, in that the body, from its nature, is always divisible and the mind is completely (86) indivisible. For in reality, when I consider the mind—that is, when I consider myself in so far as I am only a thinking being—I cannot distinguish any parts, but I ⟨recognize ⌜and⟩ conceive ⟨very clearly⟩⌝ that I am a thing which is ⟨absolutely⟩ unitary and entire. And although the whole mind seems to be united with the whole body, nevertheless when a foot or an arm or some other part ⟨of the body⟩ is amputated, I recognize quite well that nothing has been lost to my mind on that account. Nor can the faculties of willing, perceiving, understanding, and so forth be ⌜any more properly⌝ called parts of the mind, for it is ⟨one and⟩ the same mind which ⌜as a complete unit⌝ wills, perceives, and understands ⌜, and so forth⌝. But just the contrary is the case with corporeal or extended objects, for I cannot imagine any ⌜, however small they might be,⌝ which my mind does not very easily divide into ⌜several⌝ parts, and I consequently recognize these objects to be divisible. This ⟨alone⟩ would suffice to

show me that the mind ⌈or soul of man⌉ is altogether different
from the body, if I did not already know it sufficiently well
for other reasons. [69]

I also take notice that the mind does not receive impressions from all parts of the body directly, but only from the
brain, or perhaps even from one of its smallest parts—the one,
namely, where the senses in common have their seat. This
makes the mind feel the same thing whenever it is in the same
condition, even though the other parts of the body can be dif-
ferently arranged, as is proved by an infinity of experiments
which it is not necessary to describe here.

I furthermore notice that the nature of the body is such
that no one of its parts can be moved by another part some
little distance away without its being possible for it to be
moved in the same way by any one of the intermediate parts,
even when the more distant part does not act. For example,
in the cord A B C D ⌈which is thoroughly stretched⌉, if (87)
we pull ⌈and move⌉ the last part D, the first part A will not
be moved in any different manner from that in which it could
also be moved if we pulled one of the middle parts B or C,
while the last part D remained motionless. And in the same
way, when I feel pain in my foot, physics teaches me that this
sensation is communicated by means of nerves distributed
through the foot. When these nerves are pulled in the foot, being stretched like cords from there to the brain, they likewise
pull at the same time the ⟨internal⟩ part of the brain ⌈from
which they come and⌉ where they terminate, and there produce a certain movement which nature has arranged to make
my mind feel pain as though that pain were in my foot. But
because these nerves must pass through the leg, the thigh, the
loins, the back, and the neck, in order to extend from the foot
to the brain, it can happen that even when the nerve endings
in the foot are not stimulated, but only some of the ⟨inter-
mediate⟩ parts ⌈located in the loins or the neck⌉, ⟨precisely⟩
the same movements are nevertheless produced in the brain
that could be produced there by a wound received in the foot,
as a result of which it necessarily follows that the mind feels

the same pain ⌐in the foot as though the foot had been wounded⌐. And we must make the same judgment about all our other sense perceptions.

Finally, I notice that since each one of the movements that occurs in the part of the brain from which the mind receives impressions directly can only produce in the mind a single sensation, we cannot ⌐desire or⌐ imagine any better arrangement than that this movement should cause the mind to feel that sensation, of all the sensations the movement is [70] capable of causing, which is most effectively and frequently useful for the preservation of the human body when it is in full health. But experience shows us that all the sensations which nature has given us are such as I have just stated, and therefore there is nothing in their nature which does not show the power and the goodness of ⌐the⌐ God ⌐who has produced them⌐.

Thus, for example, (88) when the nerves of the foot are stimulated violently and more than is usual, their movement, passing through the marrow of the backbone up to the ⟨interior of the⟩ brain, produces there an impression upon the mind which makes the mind feel something—namely, pain as though in the foot—by which the mind is ⌐warned and⌐ stimulated to do whatever it can to remove the cause, taking it to be very ⌐dangerous and⌐ harmful to the foot.

It is true that God could establish the nature of man in such a way that this same brain event would make the mind feel something quite different; for example, it might cause the movement to be felt as though it were in the brain, or in the foot, or else in some other ⟨intermediate⟩ location ⌐between the foot and the brain⌐, or finally it might produce any other feeling ⌐that can exist⌐; but none of those would have contributed so well to the preservation of the body ⌐as that which it does produce⌐.

In the same way, when we need to drink, there results a certain dryness in the throat which affects its nerves and, by means of them, the interior of the brain. This brain event makes the mind feel the sensation of thirst, because under those conditions there is nothing more useful to us than to know that we need to drink for the conservation of our health. And similar reasoning applies to other sensations.

From this it is entirely manifest that, despite the supreme goodness of God, the nature of man, in so far as he is composed of mind and body, cannot escape being sometimes ⌈faulty and⌉ deceptive. For if there is some cause which produces, not in the foot, but in some other part of the nerve which is stretched from the foot to the brain, or even in the brain ⌈itself⌉, the same effect which ordinarily occurs when the foot is injured, we will feel pain as though it were in the foot, and we will naturally be deceived by the sensation. The reason for this is that the same brain event can cause only a single sensation in the mind; and this [71] sensation being much more frequently produced by a cause which wounds the foot than by another acting in a different location, it is much more reasonable (89) that it should always convey to the mind a pain in the foot rather than one in any other part ⌈of the body⌉. And if it happens that sometimes the dryness of the throat does not come in the usual manner from the fact that drinking is necessary for the health of the body, but from some quite contrary cause, as in the case of those afflicted with dropsy, nevertheless it is much better that we should be deceived in that instance than if, on the contrary, we were always deceived when the body was in health; and similarly for the other sensations.

And certainly this consideration is very useful to me, not only so that I can recognize all the errors to which my nature is subject, but also so that I may avoid them or correct them more easily. For knowing that each of my senses conveys truth to me more often than falsehood concerning whatever is useful or harmful to the body, and being almost always able to use several of them to examine the same object, and being in addition able to use my memory to bind and join together present information with what is past, and being able to use my understanding, which has already discovered all the causes of my errors, I should no longer fear to encounter falsity in the objects which are most commonly represented to me by my senses.

And I should reject all the doubts of these last few days as exaggerated and ridiculous, particularly that very general uncertainty about sleep, which I could not distinguish from waking life. For now I find in them a very notable difference, in that our memory can never bind and join our dreams together ⌜one with another and all⌝ with the course of our lives, as it habitually joins together what happens to us when we are awake. And so, in effect, if someone suddenly appeared to me when I was awake and ⌐afterward¬ disappeared in the same way, as ⌜do images that I see⌝ in my sleep, so that I could not determine where he came from or where he went, it would not be without reason that I would consider it a ghost (90) or a phantom produced in my brain ⌜and similar to those produced there when I sleep⌝, rather than truly a man.

But when I perceive objects in such a way that I distinctly recognize both the place from which they come and the place where they are, as well as the time when they appear to me; and when, without any hiatus, I can relate my perception of them with all the rest of my life, I am entirely certain that I perceive them wakefully and not in sleep. And I should not in any way doubt the truth of these things [72] if, having made use of all my senses, my memory, and my understanding, to examine them, nothing is reported to me by any of them which is inconsistent with what is reported by the others. For, from the fact that God is not a deceiver, it necessarily follows that in this matter I am not deceived.

But because the exigencies of action frequently ⌜oblige us to make decisions and⌝ do not ⌜always⌝ allow us the leisure to examine these things with sufficient care, we must admit that human life is very often subject to error in particular matters; and we must in the end recognize the infirmity ⌜and weakness⌝ of our nature.